D0937372

Demand, Supply, and the Market Mechanism

Richard E. Hattwick
Associate Professor of Economics
Western Illinois University

Joel W. Sailors
Associate Professor of Economics
University of Houston

Bernard G. Brown
Associate Professor of Economics
Sangamon State University

PRENTICE-HALL, INC.,
Englewood Cliffs, New Jersey

© 1971
by PRENTICE-HALL, INC.
Englewood Cliffs, New Jersey

All rights reserved.
No part of this book may
be reproduced in any form
or by any means without
permission in writing from
the publisher.

13–197996–5

Library of Congress
Catalog Card Number: 76–149979

Current printing (last digit):

10 9 8 7 6 5 4 3 2 1

Prentice-Hall International, Inc., *London*
Prentice-Hall of Australia, Pty. Ltd., *Sydney*
Prentice-Hall of Canada, Ltd., *Toronto*
Prentice-Hall of India Private Limited, *New Delhi*
Prentice-Hall of Japan, Inc., *Tokyo*

Printed in the United States of America

Preface

The basic premise of this work is that the simple analytics of supply and demand can and should be applied to study innumerable different economic problems without getting bogged down in the rigorous details of more sophisticated analytical tools. Most economists would agree with this view, but there does not currently exist a textbook that adequately presents this approach for student use. In filling this gap, the authors hope to provide the reader with a number of unifying principles which will make the study of economics easier, more interesting, and more successful.

The present volume is directed at four audiences. For the serious student in an introductory course, the chapters which follow should provide supplementary reading enlarging upon the nature of the market process in its role as a social decision-making system. For the student in an intermediate microeconomic theory course, this text should serve as a welcome supplement to basic texts by clarifying a number of often neglected issues. For the graduate student, the present volume should prove helpful in providing a framework within which the highly rigorous analyses of advanced microeconomic analysis can be placed in perspective. And for any college graduate who is curious about the fundamental nature of the market process, this volume should provide a welcome perspective.

The chapters which follow are designed to supplement existing treatments of microeconomic theory by providing several emphases usually omitted by traditional texts. One of these emphases is that of the multiple and often conflicting economic objectives which are simultaneously pursued by the participants in the market process. Microeconomic theory has always recognized the existence of conflict,

but most currently popular treatments of the economic problem restrict the discussion to a broadly defined concept of allocative efficiency. Recent work in the applied field of industrial organization and
public policy suggests that any attempt to evaluate the performance
of actual markets will benefit from a consideration of other goals,[1]
and the chapters which follow attempt to provide the reader with an
introduction to this new, policy-oriented approach.

A second unusual feature of the present volume is the emphasis
on general equilibrium analysis. Throughout the chapters which follow, the analysis focuses upon the interrelationship of markets. The
emphasis is upon the dynamic interaction of the components of the
market system and no attempt is made to discuss a complete general
equilibrium model in terms of such traditional topics as the existence
or uniqueness of a general equilibrium. But the authors believe that
the major contribution which general equilibrium analysis has to make
to economic thinking is the emphasis upon the interrelatedness of
markets and that is where the emphasis is placed on this text.

The stress upon dynamic adjustment processes represents a
third area in which the present volume complements existing texts.
Most of the latter give little attention to the dynamic adjustment
mechanisms which yield the equilibrium states upon which most of
the micro-analysis is constructed. To be sure, one encounters brief
discussions of the cobweb model, Walras' *tâtonnement,* or, a Marshallian process. But such presentations are not given the central place
found in the chapters which follow.

A fourth distinction between the present volume and orthodox
texts is the discussion of social goods. This discussion, found in the
final chapter, follows naturally from the policy-oriented emphasis of
the remaining chapters. Public production or public finance are not
the only alternatives to the competitive market process, but insofar as
the purposes of the present volume are concerned it is sufficient to
call the reader's attention to the existence of alternatives and the
necessity of resorting to such alternatives for the production of some
goods and services even when much decision-making has been delegated to the market.

The concept of economic markets and the categorization of

---

[1] See, for example: R. Caves, *American Industry: Structure, Conduct,
Performance,* Englewood Cliffs, N.J., Prentice-Hall, 1967; and M. Massel,
Monopoly and Competition, Washington, The Brookings Institution, 1962.

market forces as either supply or demand forces underlay all economic analysis and the reader who has mastered these concepts will be better prepared to do relatively sophisticated economic analysis.

R. E. H.
J. W. S.
B. G. B.

Contents

1 The Origin of Markets and Firms   1

2 The Market Solution
       to the Problem of Resource Allocation   15

3 The Market Solution
       to the Problem of Economic Growth   43

4 The Market Solution
       to the Problem of Income Distribution   67

5 The Market Solution
       to the Problem of Economic Instability   97

6 The Need for Nonmarket Solutions:
       Market Imperfections and Public Goods   115

       Conclusion   132

       Index   135

1

The
Origin
of Markets
and Firms

Having a concept of a "market" is a crucial step toward understanding all the material that follows. A "market" can be loosely defined as the "place" where the price of a product is determined. The mechanisms by which this occurs and the social implications of the price determination process are the concern of the remaining chapters. Hence, it is desirable to begin our study with a rudimentary review of the reasons for the existence of markets.[1] What follows is part fact and part fiction; but, if imagined as fact, it will serve admirably as a vehicle for understanding why all modern economies are organized as they are.

THE BASES OF SPECIALIZATION AND TRADE

The Self-Sufficient Pioneer

In the seventeenth and eighteenth centuries, the overwhelming majority of the people in what is now the eastern part of the United States were principally farmers, oftentimes living miles apart. It will serve our purpose best if we assume that all persons were farmers

---

[1] This approach has a venerable history. Adam Smith, the intellectual founder of our science, used this approach in his seminal work, *An Inquiry into the Causes and Consequences of the Wealth of Nations* (1776). Since that time, academic specialization has caused much of the material contained in this chapter to be removed from courses in microeconomic theory. Hence, students using this text as a supplementary text in a microeconomic theory course should find this a welcome review.

who lived miles apart and that each person made every item he consumed. This state of affairs results in a so-called nonmarket economy.

Typically, a person would move to virgin land in order to establish himself as a farmer. His first task was to clear the land of timber and stones so that cultivation could be undertaken. However, this task was not without benefit, for this pioneer would notch the fallen trees and stack them in the form of squares and/or rectangles, which formed the walls of his log cabin. Other logs could be used to form the roof and the floor if he decided a dirt floor were not desirable. Also, the logs could be used to form fences and out buildings. Of course, the logs could be split and the resultant lumber could be used for the above purposes to give a dressier look and more efficient structures. Consequently, our forefathers were not only farmers but carpenters as well.

If this pioneer wanted to heat the cabin as well as furnishing some light at night and a place to cook his meals indoors, he would use the stones obtained from clearing the land to construct a fireplace. This pioneer was, therefore, a farmer, carpenter, and a rock mason.

In the event that the pioneer desired a more portable light than that furnished by the fireplace in order to light the recesses of the cabin, our pioneer would make his own candles by obtaining the wax from a plant or tree, melting it and forming it around a piece of string. To his other occupations would be added that of candlemaker.

Two features of the above type of activity are apparent—the pioneer was a "jack-of-all-trades," and he obtained every item he used by wresting it from his natural surroundings.

The pioneer also obtained his clothing and food in much the same fashion. He gathered wild fruits and berries for consumption as well as the leaves of some plants to make a salad or to be cooked as greens. In addition, of course, he cultivated some food crops. He fished and hunted for the meat that furnished his dinner table. For clothing, this pioneer could obtain materials in several ways, but one method was to remove the protective coats from animals and use the skins. Thus, our pioneer not only wanted a bear, for example, for his meat and tallow but also for his skin. Of course, merely hollowing out a bear and stepping inside his outer covering left the pioneer with an ill-fitting costume. Consequently, he had to perform a bit of tailoring. To obtain a hat the individual had only to find and process a 7⅛ size raccoon. Shoes could also be fashioned from the animal skins by cutting the skin to a certain size, folding it over to shape the foot, and holding the shape with thongs also cut from the animal skin. For finer clothes, the pioneer might grow cotton or flax or raise sheep, but the methods to produce material were more indirect and time-consuming since the fibers would have to be combed, spun into thread, woven into cloth, cut, and then sewed into clothing. Dyeing of cloth was done by using, for example, certain barks, leaves, or roots. So, to the growing list of occupations one may add hunter, fisherman, tailor, hatter, shoemaker, and dyer.

Naturally, all this rough and dirty work and clothing resulted in our pioneer being in a state that could be described as "gamey." Of necessity, the pioneer became a soapmaker by using some of the previously obtained bear grease, mixing it with ashes from the fireplace, possibly adding a little sand, boiling the mixture, and letting it harden.

Another feature of this nonmarket economy is that the level of living of the pioneer depended primarily on his desire to work as well as on the bounty of nature. That is, given nature's supply, the harder and more effectively this individual worked, the greater his stock of earthly goods.

The family was both the unit of production and the unit of consumption in this economy. The family offered room for "granny," small children, and the "idiot" brother; for, if they were able to produce their share, they were no burden. Most of the tasks mentioned above could be effectively performed by almost anyone within the tolerances acceptable in those rough and simple days. Small children could gather fruits and berries, collect firewood, and perform many other necessary tasks. The same was true with respect to grandparents. All this contributed to mutual respect and affection among the family since all were contributing to a common cause except those severely handicapped because of age, mentality, and/or physical condition.

In this simple economy there was no need for social security, unemployment insurance, mental institutions, as well as many other modern "necessities" including the presence of governments in order that the economy continue to perform in its usual form. Additionally, these pioneers were not plagued by juvenile delinquency, for among several reasons was the simple problem that it was difficult, if not impossible, for youths of like mind to learn of such behavior when they were separated by miles of space, worked from dawn to dusk, and faced the additional task of finding property or persons other than their own to violate. No wonder the physiocratic notion of the moral value of a rural life assumed such currency since it was almost physically impossible to act otherwise.

To demonstrate that organizing an economy in such a fashion could not conceivably produce a modern standard of living is not difficult. All one has to do is to imagine everyone trying to wrest from Mother Nature one ubiquitous item in a modern home—a television set. A television set cannot be hunted, harvested, picked, cultivated, or mined; it does not appear in its final form as a creation of Nature, nor can you easily form it from two or three things that are extracted by the above processes. First, one would be required to go to a deposit of sand of acceptable quality, mine it, and take it to a forest. Then one would have to fell many trees and build a nice fire to melt the sand while blowing the huge glass bubble into the required shape and size for the television picture tube. After this had been accomplished, one would need to coat the inside of the tube with some aluminum. This task would require a trip to Bauxite County, Arkansas to obtain some of its red earth. Upon returning one would then have to build the hottest wood fire known to man (in fact, this would not suffice) in order to reduce the dirt to aluminum metal. If the set requires rubber, a trip would be made to South America to locate and tap a rubber tree.

Simple Specialization and Exchange

It can be plainly seen that accomplishing the above three tasks alone would require many years of undivided attention and effort if they could, indeed, be completed in any case. Our self-sufficient pioneers could set themselves on a path leading to a modern standard of living by a very simple change in their economic order. Once this change is made and widely accepted, not only will standards of living *immediately* rise but there will also occur profound changes in social and political life.

This simple change in the economic order involves the abandonment of the task of directly producing each and every item of each person's or family's consumption requirements in favor of each family or person specializing in production and trading some of this specialty product to others for their specialty product.

This can be demonstrated very simply by assuming that we

have only two pioneers or families (Smith and Jones) and that they only produce two things for themselves—soap and candles. Further, assume that the working day is uniform throughout the year and is equally divided where each family makes soap in the morning and candles in the afternoon. The Smith family may regularly make four bars of soap in the morning and five candles in the afternoon while the Jones family makes five bars of soap and three candles during those same periods.

By coincidence, Mr. Smith and Mr. Jones may meet in the course of their work. Mr. Smith may have conceived of himself as a very proficient soap maker and is amazed to find that the Jones family produces more but that the Smith family is better in candle production. This situation is summarized in tabular form:

TABLE 1–1

Unspecialized Production and Levels of Living

| Family | Products | |
	Soap	Candles
Smith	4	5
Jones	5	3
GNP	9	8

It will be noticed that the total daily production of the two is nine bars of soap and eight candles, and, if these are the only people in this country, the figures are the Gross National Product for that day. The Smith's daily level of living consists of four bars of soap and five candles.

In their discussion, Smith and Jones—being intelligent—arrive at an agreed upon novel experiment. Let the Smith family make candles in the morning and the afternoon while the Jones family devotes the day to soap making and at the end of the day meet and exchange with each other all the extra soap and candles produced with the additional one-half day applied by each to their production. If they so specialize in production, notice what happens to total production in this economy—it increases from nine soaps and eight candles to ten soaps and ten candles as seen in Table 1–2.

TABLE 1–2

Specialized Production

| | Products | |
Family	Soap	Candles
Smith	—	10
Jones	10	—
GNP	10	10

Total production has increased tremendously by this simple change even though there exists the same effort and knowledge on the part of Smith and Jones. GNP is very likely to increase even more because each family will "learn by doing" (technological progress). For example, Jones will become more adept at soap making by continual repetition of his tasks, and he is likely to subdivide the tasks to members of his family who will all become more proficient as a result.

According to the conditions of their agreement, Smith and Jones meet at the end of the day and exchange the half-day output of their specialized product. That is, Jones keeps five bars of soap, which he normally made in the morning and brings five bars of soap that he made that afternoon. Smith keeps five candles and brings the morning production of five candles to the meeting with Jones. Smith trades his five candles for the five bars of soap Jones made that morning. The result for the level of living is given in Table 1–3.

Compare the levels of living of Smith and Jones in the unspecialized and specialized production cases illustrated by Tables 1–1

TABLE 1–3

Specialized Level of Living

| | Products | |
Family	Soap	Candles
Smith	5	5
Jones	5	5
GNP	10	10

and 1–3. Smith has as many candles as before but has an extra bar of soap while Jones has the same number of soaps but has two additional candles. Clearly, both Smith and Jones are better off by specializing in production and trading for their unspecialized product. Thus, specialization and exchange has not only increased total output instantly but has immediately raised the levels of living of all. Where this exchange of soap and candles takes place we have what is called a market place, about which more will be said presently.

Smith and Jones have more goods under this arrangement, but they could make other choices. For example, they may reduce the number of hours of the day that they work in specialization to give them exactly the same level of living as before. This could be done by reducing the GNP to nine soaps and eight candles, which would allow Jones to reduce his hours of work by 10 percent and Smith to reduce his by 20 percent. Another alternative for Smith and Jones would be to reduce their work day less than the above percentage and have more goods and leisure at the same time. In fact, historical statistics amply demonstrate that people choose the latter.

Reviewing the trade made by Smith and Jones, one might conclude that Jones got the better deal since he increased his standard of living by 2 candles while Smith increased his by 1 soap. By trading 5 bars of soap for 5 candles the terms of trade are at a ratio of 1 bar of soap to 1 candle. We arbitrarily chose these terms of trade, but, in fact, it is a matter of bargaining in the market place as to the terms of trade. However, the actual figure has upper and lower limits established by Jones and Smith. For example, Smith would not take less than 4 bars of soap for his 5 candles ($\frac{4}{5}$ soap to 1 candle), for he alone could make 4 bars of soap in the morning and 5 candles in the afternoon and be better off than specializing and trading at the above terms of trade. Likewise, Jones would never give up to Smith as many as 5 bars of soap for 3 candles ($1\frac{2}{3}$ soaps to 1 candle), for he could himself make 5 bars of soap in the morning and 3 candles in the afternoon and be better off. Thus, to make both Jones and Smith participate in this arrangement they *will* agree to a trade between $\frac{4}{5}$ soaps for 1 candle and $1\frac{2}{3}$ soaps for 1 candle to the mutual benefit of the two. The terms of trade are the prices of soap and candles in terms of each other. The actual terms of trade (prices) at the market place will depend on the strengths of relative desires of Smith and Jones for soap and candles. For example, if Smith values candles over soap more strongly than Jones, he will insist that he get more soap for a candle while Jones is inclined to give it to him so that the terms of trade will be nearer $1\frac{2}{3}$ soaps for 1 candle than $\frac{4}{5}$ soap for 1 candle.[2]

This example involves two people, but the principle applies to geographic regions also. That is, one could insert the states of Maine and California in place of Smith and Jones, and the logic involving the superiority of specialization and exchange between California and Maine over nonspecialization applies equally. Or one could use countries in place of Smith and Jones. Thus, trade between the United States and Cuba or between the Soviet Union and Albania could be analyzed in this fashion. Individuals and countries that fail to take advantage of this principle do so at the cost of working longer for a lower standard of living. That is, an opportunity cost is accepted and borne, and it is an example of what is called economic inefficiency.

However, in our illustration, the economic gains in more soap and candles and/or more leisure are gross gains. It takes effort and/or time (a cost) for Smith and Jones to agree to meet, to come together with their soap and candles, and to return with the other product. For example, suppose that this daily exchange (marketing) requires 20 percent of the working day of both parties in which case there would be no advantage for Smith to specialize and exchange, whereas it would become disadvantageous for Jones since the time he saved amounted to only 10 percent of the working day. Smith would be indifferent to the arrangement while Jones would refuse to participate, which would mean that each would return to the old ways of production. The new way would also have lowered GNP by two bars of soap and two candles to the figures of eight soaps and eight candles, which is less than the original unspecialized production output for the two combined. That is, marketing is a cost, an overhead, that does not contribute to the production of soap or candles and must be borne if specialization and exchange occur; and, therefore, this cost must be subtracted from the gross gains of specialized production.

All is not lost, however. If we can reduce the costs of marketing by saving time and effort, this will allow Smith and Jones to use that

[2] Our example illustrates the so-called "Law of Absolute Advantage" where Smith is a "better" candlemaker than Jones, but Jones is a "better" soapmaker. It would also pay both Smith and Jones to specialize and exchange if either is both a better soapmaker and candlemaker than the other. This line of reasoning, known as the "Law of Comparative Advantage" is explained in virtually every introductory economics text as well as in all texts in international trade economics.

saved time to continue producing soap and candles. One possible way would be for them to agree to meet for marketing once every five days. Thus, the 20 percent of one day's cost of marketing is not borne *every* day but every fifth day, which means GNP for the five days would be forty-eight bars of soap and forty-eight candles compared to the unspecialized total production for the five day period of forty-five bars of soap and forty candles. In this case, the gross gains in production are not wiped out by excessive marketing costs, and both Smith and Jones would profit. The improvement in marketing efficiency may have resulted from improving their *transportation* to the meeting place, such as using animals instead of walking with their wares. This is another example of technological progress.

Suppose Jones unavoidably could not meet on the appointed fifth day, which would mean Smith loses production time and no exchange occurs. Now Smith and Jones have the further difficulty of reestablishing physical contact and making a new agreement on meeting time and place. This means more lost time and lost production that could more than equal the production gains with smooth and uninterrupted marketing. Again, all is not lost. If the next time Jones could not meet he could send smoke signals to Smith not to come to the market but to continue to work and if Jones could later start a dialogue of smoke signals resulting in a new meeting time for the two, there would be no lost production. Consequently, an improvement in *communications* (technological progress)—use of smoke signals by each instead of direct and verbal methods—can *indirectly* result in increased output and standards of living; or, rather, less loss of time for actual production will allow Smith and Jones to profitably specialize and exchange.

From the foregoing another point emerges, namely, that when Smith and Jones failed to meet, Smith got a little dirtier than usual since he did not receive his soap from Jones on time while the Jones household experienced more darkness than usual. By specializing and exchanging Smith and Jones are no longer self-reliant but have to cooperate, for they are now *dependent* on one another for a higher standard of living.

FIRMS

As more and more people are brought into the specialization and exchange (market) economy, this allows for *groups* of individuals to compare skills as groups. For example, we may find that our original Smith and Jones *together* making candles for half a day and soap for half a day would produce a certain number of soaps and candles. When they compare their production with two other people, they discover that they should specialize in soap making and trade soap for candles with the other two to the mutual benefit of both groups and that this arrangement is better than Smith and Jones specializing as in the first instance and the other two people specializing and trading in candles and soap between just themselves. If this process happens naturally, as it will, the more efficient candlemakers will combine production as will the soapmakers.

Individuals within the soap-making group will subspecialize in *part* of the process of making soap by subdividing the tasks more efficiently, and many types of savings in time, effort, and materials up to a certain point will be forthcoming. All involved can benefit from the increased production. From this process, candle- and soap-making firms emerge.

As the firms grow, they look for ways to make production more efficient—less costly in terms of effort and time—such as the introduction of machinery and an emphasis on higher labor skills. This emphasis on efficiency on the production side means that some or most family members, such as small children and older people, become less suitable as workers. The tendency then is that only the most efficient member of a family works so that the producing and consuming units are now different. The use of money (see below) also enables firms to hire labor for money wages. Family ties are not as strong as in the unspecialized economy. Further, there is a greater difficulty in the impersonal market place in matching the right kinds and amount of production to the consumption wishes of other consumption units.

MONEY

As the number of individuals and products involved in the market process increases, there arises a need for a commodity that can serve as a standard of exchange value for all goods and services and that lends itself to ready use in day-to-day transactions. These are two of the functions performed by money. Hence, it should be no surprise to discover that with the growth of specialization and exchange, money and monetary systems will evolve.

When trade was limited to the exchange of soap and candles between Jones and Smith, there was little need for money. The exchange values of soap and candles could easily be stated in terms of one another. Both Jones and Smith could take their products to market with a full knowledge of what other product would be available in exchange and at approximately what ratios of exchange. Such knowledge would naturally evolve out of repeated dealings with one another. Under these circumstances, Smith and Jones would be quite content to barter—that is, to exchange their two products directly for one another without the use of money.

But as additional traders and products become involved, exchange on a barter basis becomes increasingly inconvenient. For example, Smith may want to exchange his candles for some of Jones's soap, as well as for potatoes that a third party, Wilson, is willing to trade. But Wilson may not want any of Smith's candles. Wilson may only be interested in Jones's soap. In this case, Smith's course of action might be to exchange all his candles for Jones's soap and then take some of the newly acquired soap and exchange it for Wilson's potatoes.

As the number of persons and products involved in such a process increases, barter becomes increasingly cumbersome and time-consuming, and the participants in the market process become increasingly willing to sell their wares for a commodity that is widely accepted in exchange and that maintains relatively stable exchange ratios with respect to most other commodities. This "money" may be a precious metal, a sea shell, a piece of paper printed by a government, or anything else that traders will accept.

The spread of the use of money will encourage additional specialization by reducing the time and risk involved in marketing the product. Money will also promote specialization by encouraging the growth of firms employing numerous individuals, because the firm's organizers will find potential employees much more willing to specialize in return for a money payment than would be the case if the organizer promised to pay employees with a portion of the firm's physical product. Thus, money serves as a particularly valuable means of deferred payment because, unlike other means of deferred payment, money has generalized purchasing power.

Money also facilitates specialization and exchange by making the investment process easier. For example, money can be used to accumulate a store of purchasing power that can then be used to build a specialized soap factory, to equip it with machinery, and to train employees to use the machinery. Until the factory actually begins to produce and sell soap, the persons investing in it will receive nothing in exchange for the resources that they have committed. Instead, these investors will be drawing down assets that they had accumulated as the result of market exchanges in the past.

Money is not the only form in which a store of purchasing power can be accumulated. Jones could accumulate a stock of soap and attempt to use it to pay workers to build a soap factory. But money has the advantage of being readily accepted in exchange, and this undoubtedly encourages accumulation as long as the value of money is relatively stable over time.

Money also facilitates investment by making it easier for savers and investors to locate one another. Chapter 3 discusses the process by means of which market economies encourage those who wish to save to loan their idle purchasing power to those who wish to invest. Such exchanges could take place in a barter economy, but the magnitudes would be much smaller due to the fact that, in the absence of money, the borrower (investor) would be unable to promise the lender (saver) a return in terms of a commodity that would be widely and readily accepted in exchange. Hence, the risk assumed by the lender would be compounded.

The introduction of money into the economy also adds to the complexity of economic analysis by creating a distinction between monetary phenomena and real phenomena. An earlier generation of economists faced this problem by concentrating on the "real" phenomena, arguing that money is merely a veil that should be lifted in order to reveal the underlying fundamental facts of economic life. Modern economists recognize this view to be too simple. Monetary phenomena are now seen as forming a fundamental part of economic reality. This issue, however, lies far beyond the scope of the present work.[3]

SUMMARY

Markets arise because of the opportunities for increasing labor productivity through specialization of production. If such specialization is to succeed, opportunities for exchange must be created, and

[3] Those interested in pursuing the topic of money should consult the literature in the areas of macroeconomics and money and capital markets.

this is the role of the market. The specialization may consist of single individuals producing complete goods or services that are then sold in the market. But frequently, the gains from specialization will be such that groups of individuals will work together to produce a single product. This new organization, the business firm, then becomes the seller in the market. As specialization progresses, an important new phenomenon—money—makes its appearance and facilitates the process of specialization.

Specialization, the firm, and the exchange of goods and services for one another through the medium of money—these are key institutions in what is called the market economy. Having placed these in perspective, we now turn to an analysis of the ways in which established market economies solve fundamental economic problems.

2

The

Market

Solution

to the

Problem

of Resource

Allocation

Trade, specialization, and the firm are basic to all modern economies. But one type of economy, the market economy, has dominated economic analysis in the English-speaking countries. Faithfully adhering to this tradition, this text will concentrate upon the decision-making processes that constitute the "purely competitive" market system.[1]

Market systems are both amazingly easy to understand and exceedingly complex to describe. They are easy to understand because simple "models" of such systems manage to retain the essential properties of the more complex real world working systems. This suggests that we begin by examining one of these simple models, leaving the more complicated cases for later scrutiny.

The present chapter describes the manner in which a purely competitive market system would solve the problem of allocating "scarce resources" among "unlimited alternative uses." The first part illustrates the nature of the problem of scarcity by constructing our first analytical tool, the production possibilities curve. The second section describes the mechanism whereby demand and supply in a market determine the level of output. The third section explains how

---

[1] Throughout this book we will encounter terms that (1) have a specialized meaning in economic analysis, a meaning that students will not fully appreciate, and (2) will not be defined until sometime after the term has been introduced. Such terms will normally be enclosed between quotation marks the first time they are encountered. This technique of using terms having specialized meanings without defining them is highly objectionable from a heuristic point of view. But for pedagogical "overview" purposes this approach is useful, as long as the context and everyday meaning of the term are together sufficient to allow the student to follow the main lines of the argument.

supply and demand, working simultaneously in all markets, determine where on the production possibilities curve the economy will produce. Finally, the fourth section points out the social welfare implications of this competitive process.

THE PRODUCTION POSSIBILITIES CURVE

A simple yet effective way of illustrating the problem of scarcity is to construct a production possibilities curve. Such a curve shows the various combinations of goods and services that the economy can produce when at least one of its "scarce" factors of production is being fully utilized.

Construction of a Production Possibilities Curve

Let us suppose, for example, that we have an economy in which the following assumptions hold:

1. Only two commodities are produced, these being cloth and corn, and these commodities are produced under conditions of pure competition (a large number of buyers and sellers with all sellers offering identical products and with free entry into the market).
2. Labor is the only "scarce" factor of production.
3. All units of labor are equally productive in the production of either cloth or corn. One worker will produce one bushel of food or one yard of cloth per year.
4. The labor supply consists of one thousand men.
5. Wants are unlimited.
6. Sellers do not hold inventories.

Given these conditions, we can construct the production possibilities curve by hypothetically moving labor from the production of cloth to that of corn and by observing the changes in output of each item. Thus, as suggested by Table 2–1, if all the available labor is devoted to the production of corn, the annual rate of production of food would be 1000 bushels per year. If one worker is removed from corn production and directed to produce cloth, corn output will fall to 999 bushels per year while cloth production rises to one yard. If an additional worker is moved from the corn industry to the cloth

TABLE 2–1

Production Possibilities for Hypothetical Economy

LABOR INPUTS		COMMODITY OUTPUTS	
Number of Workers in		Number of Units of	
Cloth Industry	Corn Industry	Cloth	Corn
1000	0	1000	0
999	1	999	1
998	2	998	2
997	3	997	3
996	4	996	4
.	.	.	.
.	.	.	.
.	.	.	.
500	500	500	500
.	.	.	.
.	.	.	.
.	.	.	.
250	750	250	750
.	.	.	.
.	.	.	.
.	.	.	.
1	999	1	999
0	1000	0	1000

industry, corn output falls to 998 bushels per year while cloth output rises to two yards per year. Continuing this process, we can obtain various other combinations, some of which are also included in Table 2–1.

The complete list of the possible combinations of corn and cloth is called a production possibilities curve or frontier. Strictly speaking, this curve would have the stair-step shape suggested in Fig. 2–1a. However, for exposition, we can think of the points as being so close together that they appear to be a solid straight line to the naked eye so that only a microscopic examination would reveal the individual points. All relationships that are presented as lines or curves throughout this work, it is not to be forgotten, are of this nature. Fig. 2–1b presents the production possibilities curve under this assumption of linearity (assumption that a straight line adequately describes the production possibilities frontier). The points on this curve correspond to the combinations indicated in Table 2–1. This linear production

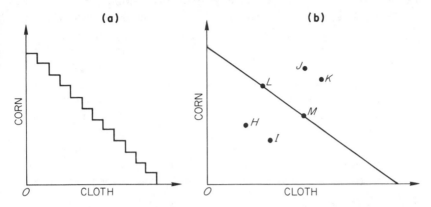

Fig. 2–1 The Production Possibilities Curve—Constant Cost Case

possibilities curve can be called the case of constant opportunity cost or the constant cost production possibilities curve.

The production possibilities curve need not take the shape of a straight line. Indeed, a more commonly encountered shape in the literature of economics is the "concave toward the origin" shape presented in Figure 2–2. This shape can be called the case of increasing opportunity cost. This curve indicates that as a successively larger proportion of the economy's scarce resources is devoted to cloth

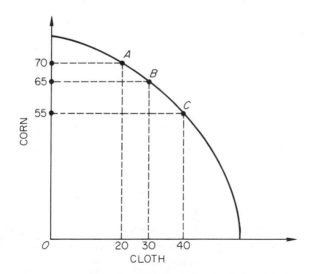

Fig. 2–2 The Production Possibilities Curve—Increasing Cost Case

production, the opportunity cost of cloth production rises. In Figure 2–2, for example, the opportunity cost of increasing cloth output by ten units from an initial output of twenty units is a cost of five units of corn. That is, the resources needed to increase cloth production by ten units could have been used to produce five units of corn. But if cloth production is at thirty units and a decision is made to increase cloth output by another ten units (to a total output, of forty), then the opportunity cost of those last ten units of cloth output will be ten units of corn. Thus, the movement from *A* to *B* on the production possibilities curve involves an opportunity cost of one-half unit of corn for each unit of cloth whereas the movement from *B* to *C* involves a higher opportunity cost of one unit of corn per unit of cloth.

The increasing opportunity cost case arises when the units of resources released from the production of one commodity are successively less productive in the production of the other commodity. If labor is the only factor of production, then the increasing opportunity cost would mean that all units of labor are not equally productive in the production of either commodity. If there are two factors of production, then the increasing opportunity cost may be due to the fact that the two commodities use the two factors of production in different proportions. Unfortunately, the proof of this proposition requires analytical tools beyond the scope of this text.

In the remainder of the present chapter, as well as in Chapter 3, the increasing opportunity cost curve will be used. However, in Chapter 4, we will return to the use of a constant opportunity cost curve or constant cost production possibilities curve.

Problems Revealed
by the Production Possibilities Curve

The production possibilities curve divides the set of all output combinations of cloth and corn into three subsets, each of which is associated with a particular economic problem. First, referring to Fig. 2–1b, there is the subset of all points below the production possibilities curve (points *H* and *I* being examples). To produce at any of these points, the economy would have to refrain from using some of the available labor. This would mean that the economy was faced with a problem of unemployed resources.

Second, there is the set of points above and to the right of the production possibilities curve (points J and K in Fig. 2–1b being examples). By definition, these are points that the economy cannot reach with its given supply of labor.[2] To reach such points, the supply of labor or its productivity must be increased. This is possible in the long run as the result of a process called economic growth. Thus, the problem of how to move into the area above the curve is the long-run problem of economic growth.

Consideration of the areas above and below the production possibilities curve quickly leads us to the conclusion that society must produce somewhere on the curve (points L and M in Fig. 2–1b being examples). This in turn leads us to the third economic problem: selecting the point on the curve at which the economy should produce.

SUPPLY AND DEMAND:
SINGLE MARKET PARTIAL EQUILIBRIUM ANALYSIS

One way of solving this problem is to delegate the decision to the forces of supply and demand in the market. Let us see how supply and demand determine the output of cloth (this technique is called single market partial equilibrium analysis). Once we have seen how supply and demand interact in the cloth market, we will be ready to discuss the process whereby supply and demand interact in both markets simultaneously (multimarket partial equilibrium analysis).

The Demand and Supply Curves

The demand curve and the supply curve for cloth are presented in Fig. 2–3. The demand curve shows the quantity of cloth that will be purchased at various prices as long as the following assumptions are accepted.[3]

1. Money income of all actual and potential purchasers is fixed.
2. Tastes do not change.

[2] This statement applies to a closed economy, that is, one that is not trading with others. By trading, an economy can reach points J or K, for example.

[3] The third assumption made here differs from that encountered in the usual text, where it is common to assume that the prices of all other goods remain constant. The reason for the use of this unorthodox assumption in the present text is that the authors are seeking to emphasize the interrelatedness of markets.

3. The prices of all other goods (corn in this case) change only in response to changes in the quantity of resources devoted to the production of cloth.

Normally, the demand curve is assumed to have a negative slope as in Fig. 2–3. The explanations for this include the probabilities

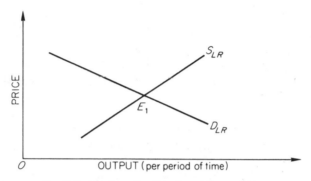

Fig. 2–3   The Long Run Supply and Demand Curves

that: (1) as the price falls, existing buyers purchase more of the product as a substitute for other goods; (2) as the price falls, existing customers can purchase more of all goods, including this good, with fixed money incomes; and (3) as the price falls, new buyers enter the market for the first two reasons. Existing textbooks in microeconomic theory develop these propositions in great detail, but the present work will be content with these plausible explanations.

The supply curve tells us what quantities of cloth will be supplied by sellers at various prices as long as the following assumptions hold:

1. Techniques of production are fixed.
2. The supply of labor for all possible uses is fixed.
3. Tastes do not change.

Normally, the supply curve is assumed to have a positive slope like the curve in Fig. 2–4. In the present case, this can be explained by the fact that as the output of one product is increased, there is a rise in the price of the other product (which is having its production reduced in order to release labor for increased production of the first product). The rising price of the foregone product represents the opportunity cost of expanding output of the first product. Hence,

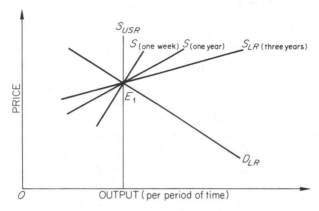

Fig. 2–4 The Three Types of Supply Curve

the opportunity cost of this first product must rise as output increases.[4]

The demand and supply curves of Fig. 2–3 differ from those found in most textbooks because of their long-run nature. In order to continually remind ourselves of this difference, we will christen these the long-run supply curve (S_{LR}) and the long-run demand curve (D_{LR}).[5]

Equilibrium—Single Market Marshallian Partial Equilibrium Analysis

A fundamental assumption of most economic analysis is that the interaction of supply and demand tends to produce an equilibrium price and output. This is the price and output at which the demand

---

[4] Another explanation of the positively sloped supply curve would be the fact that the production possibilities curve is of the increasing cost variety. In the case of the production possibilities curve, the opportunity cost is rising due to technical factors that make it increasingly difficult to transform one product into another. In the case of the rising price of the foregone other good, the rise is due to the fact that we are moving up the demand curve for that other good. That is, potential consumers are placing progressively more "value" on the foregone units.

[5] The curves that are found in most current textbooks will henceforth be referred to as the short-run supply curve and the short-run demand curve. The long-run demand curve is a locus of points on a number of orthodox short-run demand curves while the long-run supply curve is a locus of points on a series of short-run supply curves.

and supply functions intersect (E_1 in Fig. 2–3). This is called an equilibrium position because at this location the quantity demanded being equal to the quantity supplied, there are no forces that would cause the price and quantity to change.

This equilibrium position is normally assumed to be stable. That is, if, for some reason, price should rise above or fall below the equilibrium point, forces will be set in motion that will tend to return price to the equilibrium level. One method of proving this is to describe the dynamic adjustment process that tends to bring about the long-run equilibrium price. This can be done by (1) starting at one long-run equilibrium price; (2) assuming a once-and-for-all shift of the long-run demand curve; and (3) tracing out the steps by means of which the new equilibrium is established.

Before doing this, however, we must introduce two additional types of supply curves. These are the very short-run supply curve and the short-run supply curve, both of which are illustrated in Fig. 2–4. The very short-run supply curve shows how the quantity supplied will vary as the price changes, on the assumption that too little time has passed since the price change occurred to allow any adjustments on the supply side of the market. Thus, by definition, this very short-run supply curve must be perpendicular to the quantity axis and must pass through the original equilibrium point.

The short-run supply curve indicates the manner in which the supply side of the market will react once sufficient time has passed for some adjustments to be made on the supply side but before sufficient time has passed to allow all possible adjustments. For example, one week after the price has changed, sellers may be able to make the adjustments indicated by $S_{1\ \text{week}}$ (Fig. 2–4); whereas one year after the initial price change, adjustments can be made as indicated by $S_{1\ \text{year}}$; and three years after the initial price change, adjustments can be made as indicated by S_{LR}. There are, of course, a large number of short-run supply curves, each referring to a different period of time. All pass through position E_1 because this is the point of reference with respect to the analysis of dynamic adjustment process.

The phenomenon emphasized by this variety of supply curves is the time-consuming nature of adjustments on the supply side of the market. The more time allowed, the greater the adjustments that can be made. For example, if one week is allowed, there is sufficient time for existing "firms" to put on an extra shift but not sufficient time for the firms to acquire additional machinery. If one year is allowed, the machinery can be obtained but new plants cannot be completed.

If three years are allowed, there will be sufficient time to construct and put into operation the new "plants." [6] Eventually sufficient time will have passed to allow all possible adjustments on the supply side. When this occurs, we move from the short run to the long run as indicated by S_{LR}.

Having developed the additional supply curves, we are ready to describe the dynamic adjustment process depicted by Fig. 2–5. We

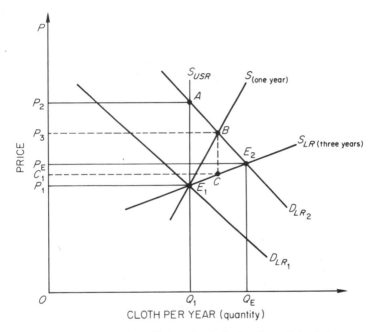

Fig. 2–5 Partial Equilibrium—Single Market, Dynamic Analysis

begin with the market in equilibrium at a price of OP_1 and output of OQ_1 (intersection of the long-run demand and supply curves). We next assume a once-and-for-all shift of the long-run demand curve to D_{LR2}. In the long run this change will result in a new equilibrium price of OP_E and output of OQ_E. This will occur as a result of the following dynamic process:

1. In the very short run there can be no output response on the supply side of the market, as is indicated by S_{VSR}. But the price can rise, and under the pressure of buyers competing for the fixed

---

[6] Note that the seller is also being treated as a producer.

quantity supplied, the price will be pushed up to OP_2 (the mechanism involved would be a variant of the bidding process discussed in Chapter 3 below).

2. The rising price enables sellers to earn more for supplying OQ_1 than was previously the case. Whereas sellers were formerly receiving a total revenue of $OP_1E_1Q_1$ for providing OQ_1, they now receive $OQAP_2$ for providing the same amount. The difference between these two sums, the rectangle $P_1E_1AP_2$, represents an amount that exceeds the suppliers' cost of production (including a "normal profit"). This windfall gain is called excess profits or quasi-rents. Its existence signals opportunities to earn above average profits for those supplying additional units of cloth to the market. Consequently, sellers already in this market make plans to increase their sales, while potential sellers make plans to enter this lucrative market.

3. By the end of one year, some of these plans have come to fruition. Existing producers have expanded the quantity they supply, and a number of new sellers have entered the market. The result is the increase in quantity supplied, indicated by the intersection of short-run supply curve $S_{1 \text{ year}}$ and the demand curve D_{LR2}. The increase in supply [7] has reduced the market price to OP_3 and increased the sellers' unit costs to OC_1. Both these developments tend to reduce quasi-rents,[8] but these rents have not been eliminated, for the rectangle C_1CBP_3 attests to the fact that sellers are still receiving a sum in excess of their "costs" of supply (including a normal profit). Hence, the market still provides opportunities for additional above average profits, and other potential sellers continue their preparations to enter the market.

4. As time passes, more and more potential sellers manage to enter the market, pushing the market price down and the costs of supplying the product up. Finally, by the end of the third year of this process of entry and expansion, the market price has been depressed to the point where it just covers the average cost of supply (including a normal profit). The incentive to expand the quantity supplied (the excess profits) has been eliminated, but there is suffi-

---

[7] Traditional textbook treatments of this process refer to any shift in the short-run supply curve as a change in supply while a movement along the short run supply curve is called a change in quantity supplied. The case of moving from a short-run supply curve of a given time period to a short-run supply curve representing a longer period has been not labeled in the literature, but we will call it a change in supply.

[8] Eventually these processes will reduce quasi-rents, but initially quasi-rents may *increase* due to favorable "price elasticities." This concept is discussed in other textbooks and will not be explored here.

cient incentive to maintain the quantity supplied at the rate OQ_E, which results in a price of OP_E. The market is once again in long-run equilibrium.

The process just described is one possible [9] dynamic process that will tend to establish a long-run equilibrium when a market is temporarily producing excess profits. A similar process may tend to bring about a long-run equilibrium when a market is temporarily suffering losses. To illustrate such a process, we turn to Fig. 2–6.

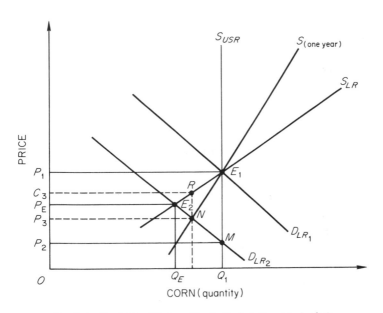

Fig. 2–6 Partial Equilibrium—Single Market, Dynamic Analysis

Starting at an initial equilibrium price of OP_1 and OQ_1 (intersection of the long-run supply curve S_{LR} and the long-run demand curve D_{LR_1}), a once-and-for-all decline in demand is introduced, this being represented by the shift of long-run demand to D_{LR_2}. This sets in motion the following dynamic process:

1. In the very short run there can be no output response on the supply side of the market, as is indicated by S_{VSR}. But the price

[9] This process is called the "Marshallian Process" after Alfred Marshall, the British economist who introduced this process in his *Principles of Economics* (1890).

can fall, and under the pressure of sellers competing to dispose of the fixed quantities they hold, the price will be pushed down to OP_2 (the mechanism involved would be a form of the bidding process described in Chapter 3 below).

2. The decline in price causes sellers to earn less for supplying OQ_1 than was previously the case. Whereas sellers were formerly receiving a total revenue of $OQ_1E_1P_1$, they are now receiving only the amount OQ_1MP_2. The difference between these two sums, the rectangle $P_2ME_1P_1$, represents the amount by which suppliers are failing to cover all their costs of production. This windfall loss is called economic loss. Its existence signals the need for some sellers to leave the market and others to cut back the quantity supplied. Consequently, sellers already in the market make plans to reduce sales and/or leave this unprofitable market.

3. By the end of one year, some of these plans have been carried out. Some of the original sellers have left this market (and entered the other market) while others have reduced the quantity supplied. The result is the decrease in the quantity supplied, which is indicated by the intersection of the short-run supply curve $S_{1 \text{ year}}$ and the demand curve D_{LR_2}. The decrease in supply causes the market price to rise to OP_3. This development tends to reduce losses, but losses have not been eliminated for the rectangle C_3RNP_3 attests to the fact that some sellers are still incurring losses. Hence, plans continue to be made for leaving the market and/or reducing the quantity supplied.

4. As time continues to pass, more and more sellers manage to leave the market, causing the quantity supplied to decrease and the market price to rise. Finally, by the end of the third year, this process of exit has pushed the price up to OP_E. At this point the price covers all the long-run average costs of supplying the quantity OQ_E. Hence, losses have been eliminated, and there is no incentive to further reduce output or leave the industry.

SUPPLY AND DEMAND: MULTIMARKET PARTIAL EQUILIBRIUM ANALYSIS

The preceding discussion dealt with supply and demand in a single market. The influence on this one market of events in other markets was assumed to be unimportant. This technique of concentrating on a single market has traditionally been called partial equilibrium analysis and is usually contrasted with general equilibrium analysis, which consists of considering *all* markets in the economy simultaneously. Like a controlled laboratory experiment, partial equilibrium analysis seeks to reduce the number of variables under observation and thereby enable us to better perceive specific interrelationships. Unfortunately, partial equilibrium analysis cannot avoid implicitly including the effects of other markets since every event in one market is associated with events in other markets.

This suggests that we look at all markets simultaneously. But such a general equilibrium analysis at this point would be unduly cumbersome. Fortunately, however, some of the economic insights derived from general equilibrium analysis can also be obtained from simultaneous consideration of several interrelated markets (as distinguished from all markets). This compromise procedure will be called multimarket partial equilibrium analysis to distinguish it from the single market partial equilibrium analysis of the preceding section.

Static Multimarket Equilibrium

One way of appreciating what this multimarket equilibrium analysis entails is to analyze the properties of a multimarket system that is in long-run equilibrium. Such an analysis is called "static" equilibrium analysis. In Fig. 2–7, such a multimarket static equilibrium model is presented. In this case, two interrelated markets—the corn market and the cloth market—are in long-run equilibrium. The corn market has an equilibrium price of P and output of twenty units per year, whereas the cloth market has an equilibrium price of P_1 and an equilibrium output of ten units per year. Assuming these two products to be the only items produced in the economy, the market equilibria select the economy's position on its production possibilities curve as indicated by position A in Fig. 2–7.

Dynamic Adjustment Process

For some purposes, the static analysis based on Fig. 2–7 would be all that was necessary to illustrate the nature of the market process. For policy purposes, however, analysis of the dynamic adjustment process is desirable. Fig. 2–8 is, in reality, a recapitulation of the processes of entry and exit portrayed by Fig. 2–5 and 2–6. All that has been added is an emphasis upon the fact that the two processes

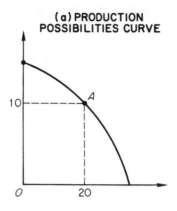

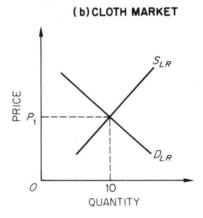

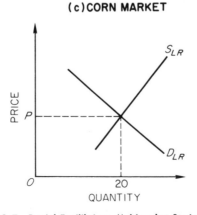

Fig. 2–7 Partial Equilibrium—Multimarket Static Analysis

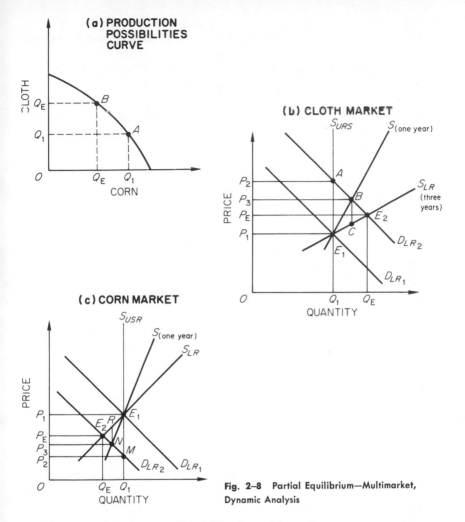

(a) PRODUCTION POSSIBILITIES CURVE

(b) CLOTH MARKET

(c) CORN MARKET

Fig. 2–8   Partial Equilibrium—Multimarket, Dynamic Analysis

are interrelated and an explicit indication of how these two processes are together responsible for the selection of the point on the production possibilities curve. That is, Fig. 2–8, maintaining the assumptions of Fig. 2–5 and 2–6, describes the following sequence of events:

1. The economy is initially in long-run equilibrium at position A on the production possibilities curve. There then occurs a once-and-for-all change in tastes, causing the demand curve in the cloth market to shift up to D_{LR_2}, and, since consumers have a fixed amount of money income to spend on cloth and corn, the demand for corn shifts down to D_{LR_2}.

2. In the very short run or market period, no adjustments can be made on the supply side of either market, but prices can change

and they do, the price in the corn market falling to OP_2 and the price in the cloth market rising to OP_2.

3. As a result of these price changes, sellers in the corn market find themselves incurring temporary losses while sellers in the cloth market find themselves enjoying windfall excess profits. As a result, sellers in the corn market make plans to reduce production and/or leave the market. Those planning to leave the market are goaded not only by the losses being incurred in the sale of corn but also by the unusually high profits to be earned in the cloth market. Thus, they plan not only to leave the corn market but also to enter the cloth market.

4. By the end of one year, some of these plans have been carried to fruition. Those already in the cloth market have expanded production and, in addition, some of those formerly in the corn market have had time to leave the market and enter the cloth market. As a result, the price of cloth has fallen, but excess profits are still being earned. In the corn market, the exit of some sellers and reduction of supply by others has caused the price to rise, but losses are still being incurred. The persistence of losses and excess profits causes sellers to continue plans to leave the corn market and enter the cloth market. (We will assume that by the end of one year, sellers in the cloth market who plan to expand cloth production have done so while sellers in the corn market who plan to stay in that market but reduce production have also done so.)

5. By the end of three years, these plans have been carried out. The process of exit from the corn industry has been carried to the point where all losses have been eliminated and the entry into the cloth industry has brought profits back to a normal level. The system is in a new long-run equilibrium. What distinguishes this equilibrium from the original one is the increased production of cloth and decreased production of corn as is indicated on the production possibilities curve by the move from A to B.

THE WELFARE IMPLICATIONS: MARKET PERFORMANCE

The competitive adjustment process is one method of selecting the point on the production possibilities curve. Having described this method, we must now inquire into the performance of this method in terms of results relevant to societal and individual well-being.

Those results of the market process that affect the well-being of members of a given society are called the performance results. In order to evaluate these performance results, we must obtain measures of desired performance in terms of each performance result. These desired performance indicators are called performance norms.

Among the performance norms that economists have identified are the following:

1. *Economic Efficiency*—According to this norm, resources should be allocated so that the "correct" items are produced in the correct quantities as desired by the consumers and with the least cost techniques of production.
2. *Economic Equity*—According to this norm, the produced goods and services should be distributed among potential users in the "correct" proportions.
3. *Economic Stability*—This norm deals with the problems of "unemployment" and "inflation." According to this norm neither long run "unemployment" nor "inflation" should exist.
4. *Economic Growth*—According to this norm, the "correct" proportion of resources should be devoted to enlarging the economy's productive capacity. This involves capital formation and innovation.
5. *Personal Security*—According to this norm, no individual should be placed in the difficult position of having his material (psychological) level of well-being suddenly diminished to any "significant" degree.

The above list is clearly inadequate for an operational evaluation of the performance results of the competitive adjustment process, because we have not stated what we mean by the word "correct." For present purposes, however, this ambiguity is acceptable.

In general, it can be said that the purely competitive market system *tends* to perform extremely well in terms of economic efficiency and fairly well in terms of economic equity and economic growth. Offsetting this good performance, however, is the distinct possibility of poor performance in terms of economic stability and personal security.

The analytical bases for most of these assertions are not presented here. However, there are two performance assertions that can be explored in closing this chapter. These are the propositions that the competitive process is efficient and that it may produce personal insecurity.

Economic Efficiency

The argument that the competitive process produces an efficient result is essentially the argument that this market process maximizes the social benefits obtained from the use of society's scarce resources. The argument takes the following form:

1. The most efficient solution is that which maximizes net total social benefits (TSB). That is, it is the solution that maximizes the excess of TSB over total social cost (TSC).

2. To maximize net TSB, society must increase production in each market where the demand price exceeds the supply price. This increase in output should continue, one unit at a time, until the price has fallen and output has risen to the point where the demand price is equal to the supply price and the quantities supplied and demanded are equal. This is so because points on the demand curve represent the amount by which gross social benefits change as output increases (this is called marginal social benefit) whereas points on the supply curve represent the amount by which total social cost changes as output increases (this is called marginal social cost). Hence, *given* the level of production, if the relevant point on the demand curve lies above that on the supply curve, then by increasing output the net total social benefits will increase since the gross change in total social benefits (or marginal social benefits) exceeds the change in total social cost (or marginal social cost).

In Fig. 2–9, for example, increasing the quantity produced from eight to nine units causes total social benefits to increase by $12 (point M on the demand curve) and total social cost to rise by $10 (point N on the supply curve). Since marginal social benefits ($12) exceed marginal social costs ($10), net social benefits increase by $2 (MSB − MSC = $12 − $10 = $2).

3. When the quantity demanded is equal to the quantity supplied and the demand price is equal to the supply price, further increases in output would cause the supply price to exceed the demand price, and this in turn would cause net social benefits to decline. In Fig. 2–9, for example, an increase in output from ten to eleven units causes total social benefits to increase by $10 (point R on the demand curve) while total social cost increased by $12 (point T on the supply curve). The net result is a decrease in net total social benefits

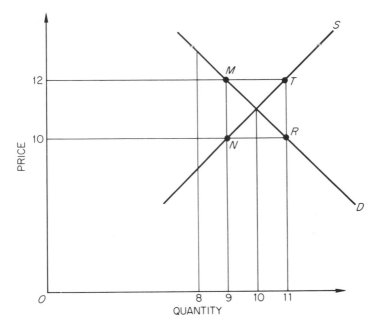

Fig. 2–9   Social Costs—Benefits in the Market

of \$2 (MSB − MSC = \$10 − \$12 = − \$2). Now if output were reduced to ten units, this decline would be eliminated. That is, net
social benefits would rise by \$2. Hence, the rule for maximizing net
total social benefits includes the dictum that whenever the supply
price exceeds the demand price, output should be reduced.

4. Thus, the maximizing rule points to the intersection of the
demand and supply curves as the position most socially desirable.

The crucial assumption in this argument is that the demand
curve is a measure of marginal social benefits while the supply curve
is a measure of marginal social cost. That is, it is assumed that the
change in total benefits accruing to a one unit increase in production
is equal to the money value placed on that unit by the consumer who
purchases it. This value, of course, is given by points on the demand
function. And it is assumed that the change in total social cost is
equal to the highest price that the same consumer would be willing
to pay for one or more units of any other good that could have been
produced if an extra unit of the good in question had been produced.
This money value is given by the supply curve.

A proper analysis of this crucial assumption requires far more sophisticated tools than those presented in the present text. Yet for our purposes, the assumption is adequate. Chapter 6 of this text will consider one major problem with this assumption—the divergence between private costs and benefits on the one hand and social costs and benefits on the other.

In passing it might be noted that the preceding paragraphs provide our first encounter with a very basic technique of economic analysis—marginal analysis. The marginal analysis is not usually presented in this fashion, but the essence of the technique is brought out in the discussion of social benefits and social costs. The essential feature of the marginal analysis is the identification of optimum positions by considering incremental changes in the relevant variables.

Personal Security and the Conflict Among Performance Norms

Personal security is the other performance norm that receives comment in this chapter. The process described here involves moving resources out of some employments into other uses. In order to bring this about, the market may have to force losses and unemployment upon assets and labor. These losses serve the useful function of forcing the resources to move to the preferred uses. But these losses represent personal insecurity, which the labor and asset owners must bear.

This is our second glimpse of one of the basic hard facts of economic life-conflict. Earlier, we employed the production possibilities curve to call attention to the conflict among alternative uses of scarce resources. We found that increased production of one desirable product requires a decrease in the production of some other desired product. Now, we have employed the concept of multiple performance norms. We have discovered that a process alleged to perform extremely well in terms of economic efficiency and several other norms will simultaneously perform poorly in terms of the norm of personal security. And we have noted that this conflict is not accidental, because the process of creating personal insecurity is a necessary part of the process of bringing about a more efficient allocation of resources.

SUMMARY

All economies face a problem of allocating scarce resources among unlimited wants. One method of doing this is to delegate the necessary decisions to a price system. This chapter has discussed the manner in which a purely competitive market system would solve this problem. The process by means of which equilibrium is established in a single market was discussed. This was followed by an explanation of the interrelationships among the equilibrium processes of several markets. Finally, the social welfare implications of the competitive market process were preliminarily presented.

The discussion in this chapter has been somewhat removed from many details of actual markets. Some of these matters receive careful attention in other textbooks, and others are to be found only in studies of specific industries. The present text purposely avoids such details in order to present an "overview" into which the reader can insert details derived from other sources.

APPENDIX

The Cobweb Equilibrium Process

Throughout the preceding chapter, the Marshallian equilibrium adjustment process was employed. As mentioned above, there are other equilibrium processes that could have been employed. The present appendix briefly discusses one of these, the cobweb process. This will enable the student to place the discussion of the chapter in proper perspective. Other equilibrium processes will be discussed in later chapters.

The so-called "cobweb" adjustment process occurs under purely competitive conditions when no quantity adjustments can be made on the supply side in the short run. Thus, by definition, a market subject to the cobweb phenomenon does not possess short-run supply functions—only the very short-run and the long-run supply functions are applicable.[10] As will be shown, achievement of eventual equilibrium requires several long-run adjustments. Hence, for purposes of discussion, the final equilibrium position resulting from the cobweb process will be labeled the "very long-run equilibrium."

Cobweb adjustment processes are illustrated in Fig. 2–10. In Fig. 2–10a the cobweb process reacts to a change in demand by producing a new very long-run equilibrium position, as the result of the following sequence of events:

1. Starting with an initial equilibrium position E_1, the long-run demand curve shifts to D_{LR_2}. In the very short run (and the short run), no response in terms of quantity supplied is possible, but the price can vary. Hence, competition among buyers forces the price up to OP_2.

2. Sellers, assuming that they can now sell all that they can bring to market at the new price of OP_2, make plans to increase the amount supplied. In the short run none of these plans can be carried out, but in the long run these plans lead to a quantity supplied of OQ_2.

3. When this new quantity is brought to the market, sellers discover that much of it remains unsold at the price OP_2. Since it was assumed that there was no investment in inventories, sellers must react to this excess quantity supplied (the amount AB at the price of OP_2) by bidding the price down. Hence, the price falls to OP_3 where the quantity demanded is equal to the quantity supplied in the very short run (and short run).

4. At this lower price sellers are only willing to supply OQ_3 in the long run. In the very short run and short run, they cannot reduce the quantity supplied to this level, but plans are made to do so in the long run.

5. In the long run these plans are carried out, and the quantity supplied falls to OQ_3. But this quantity falls short of the quantity demanded at price OP_3, and buyers therefore bid the price up until the quantity demanded is equal to the very short run (and short run) quantity supplied at price OP_4.

6. At this higher price of OP_4, sellers find that excess profits await increased supplies, and plans are made to provide these. Consequently, in the long run the quantity supplies rises to OQ_4.

7. But quantity OQ_4 cannot be sold at the anticipated price of

---

[10] Actually, this statement is misleading. A cobweb process could be generated in a market that contained discontinuous short-run supply functions. The absence of short-run supply curves is employed for pedagogical processes.

OP_4. Instead, sellers have to offer this amount at the lower price of OP_5 in order to clear the market (equate the quantity demanded with the very short run quantity supplied).

8. This lower price causes sellers to make plans to reduce the quantity supplied in the long run, and these plans come to pass, the quantity supplied falling.

9. This process of first producing more than can be sold at the anticipated price and then failing to produce enough to keep the price down to the anticipated level continues until the price is finally driven to OP_E. At this point, the long-run quantity demanded is just equal to the long-run quantity supplied. The market price induces the same quantity supplied, OQ_E, every period and all this quantity is purchased at the price OP_E. Hence, there are no market forces tending to cause a change in either price or quantity. The system is in "very long-run" equilibrium.

The cobweb process derives its name from the diagrammatic pattern created by joining the series of price and quantity points that the process produces. Thus, in Fig. 2–10a, the price (and quantity) goes from E_1 to A to B to C to D to F to G, etc. The lines joining these points resemble a spider's web.

The cobweb process of Fig. 2–10a produces a very long-run equilibrium position and is therefore called a convergent cobweb process. There are other possible results. One is the case of permanent oscillation as depicted in Fig. 2–10b. Here the shift of the long-run demand curve causes a movement of price and output from E_1 to A to B to C to E to A to B to C, etc. This process does not tend to bring the price and quantity closer and closer to the apparent very long-run equilibrium position E_2. Instead, price and quantity oscillate permanently about E_2. This case is appropriately named the oscillatory cobweb.

A third possibility is depicted in Fig. 2–10c. Here the initial shift of the long-run demand curve to D_{LR_2} causes the price and quantity to move from E_1 to A to B to C to D to F to G to H, etc. As time passes, the actual price and output position is moving farther and farther away from the apparent very long-run equilibrium position E_2. This case is called a divergent cobweb process. Such a process must eventually destroy itself, the violent fluctuations in price and output calling forth a radical change in the organization of the market.

The cobweb processes have several elements in common. One

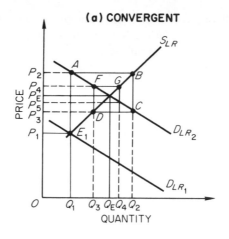

(a) CONVERGENT

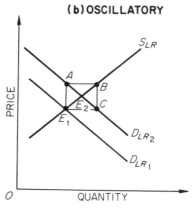

(b) OSCILLATORY

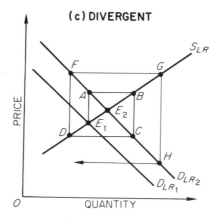

(c) DIVERGENT

Fig. 2–10   The Cobweb Process

is the long period of time that must pass before any adjustment can be made on the supply side of the market. The second is the assumption on the part of each purely competitive seller that the present price will prevail in the long run and that the seller can find buyers for any quantity offered at this price. When these conditions occur, a cobweb process is imminent.

Other types of competitive equilibrium processes include the auction, the Dutch auction, and Walrasian *tatonnement*. Noncompetitive adjustment processes include nonmarket rationing and temporal price discrimination. And, of course, both competitive and noncompetitive markets are likely to have their price fluctuations dampened by the accumulation and drawing down of inventories. All these processes must be studied for a more precise understanding of the working of the market process, but the preceding is sufficient here.

3

The

Market

Solution

to the

Problem

of Economic

Growth

The preceding chapter examined the performance of a hypothetical competitive market system where the performance measures were the norms of economic efficiency and personal security. The present section investigates the performance of such a market system in terms of another goal of public policy—economic growth.

The first part of this chapter explores the meaning of the concept of economic growth and finds the essence of growth to reside in the processes of capital formation and innovation. The second section describes the manner in which the market system determines the rate of capital formation, while the third part discusses the influence of the market system upon the rate of innovation. In the fourth part the role of the market process in determining the composition of the capital stock is explained, and the fifth part takes a look at the possible conflict between resource allocation and personal security in a growth setting. As will become apparent, the problem of growth is in many ways merely a special case of the problem of resource allocation, which was discussed in the preceding chapter.

THE GROWTH PROCESS

Economic growth is the process whereby an economy's production possibilities curve shifts "out." That is, growth is the process that leads to an increase in an economy's productive capacity. For example, in Fig. 3–1 the curve P_2P_2 represents greater productive capacity than does the curve P_1P_1. This was made possible by a

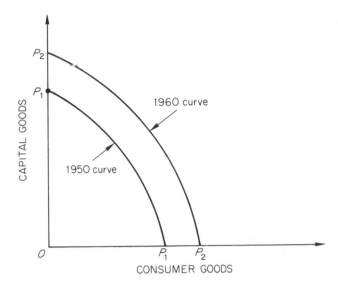

Fig. 3–1   Shifts of the Production Possibilities Curve

process of economic growth that moved the economy from curve P_1P_1 in 1950 to position P_2P_2 in 1960.

But what is the essence of this process of growth? The traditional answer given by economists was capital formation, a term synonymous with net economic investment. One of the most effective devices for laying bare the essence of this process is the circular flow model of the economic process. Fig. 3–2a presents a circular flow in static general equilibrium. In this model the economy is divided into two major sectors—the household sector and the productive sector. Four flows link these sectors. First, productive services flow from the households to the productive sector. Second, in return for providing these services, the households receive money payments from the producers. Third, the households use this money income to purchase goods and services from the productive sector. The flow of these goods and services to the households represents the fourth flow.

The kinds and amounts of goods and services comprising this fourth flow are determined by the market process described in the preceding chapter. Hence, the flow of goods and services is in equilibrium. Similarly, as will be demonstrated in the next chapter, market processes keep the flow of services from the households at equilibrium rates. Thus, the circular flow is in a long-run general equilibrium position, and there is no growth.

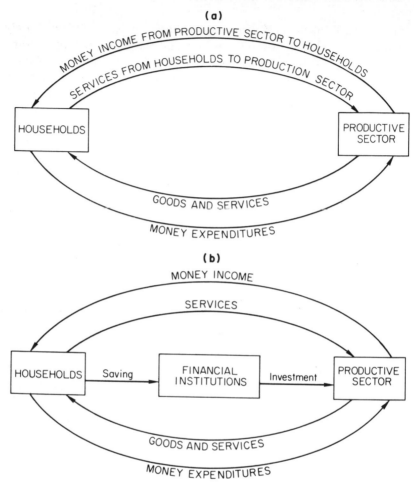

Fig. 3–2 Circular Flow

But this result arises from the failure of Fig. 3–2a to take into account the phenomenon of economic saving. This oversight is rectified in Fig. 3–2b, which portrays a portion of the flow of money income received by the households being withheld from the purchase of consumer goods and services. The resultant savings are channeled through "banks" to businesses that wish to invest in additional productive capacity, the borrowed funds being used to hire services from the households and the services being used to produce additional machine tools, factories, or other "capital goods." This is the essence of the capital formation process.

The mere existence of investment does not mean that growth is taking place, for the newly created productive capacity may be barely sufficient to replace existing capacity that has worn out or become obsolete.[1] If this were the case, then we would still have a growthless economy in static, general equilibrium. If however, the newly created capacity were more than sufficient to replace the worn out and obsolete capacity, then the economy's total productive capacity would be increased and growth would occur.

Thus, the circular flow model reveals the essence of the growth process as consisting of the generation of a "sufficient" volume of savings (foregoing consumption) and the channeling of this savings into investment (creating new capacity). These decision-making tasks were assigned to the market in the "classical" competitive economy. Hence, our next task is to describe the manner in which the market determines the amount of savings and investment.

MARKET DETERMINATION
OF THE RATE OF CAPITAL FORMATION

Market equilibrium processes determine the rates of saving and investment. These processes make the quantity of loanable funds demanded (investment) equal to the quantity of loanable funds supplied (saving). Thus, to construct a model of this market decision process, we need to construct the demand and supply functions and to describe the dynamic adjustment process that tends to bring about equilibrium.

The Demand for Loanable Funds
to be Used for Capital Formation

If it is assumed that a single market handles all the funds borrowed for purposes of economic investment in the economy, then the demand for investable funds schedule portrays an inverse relationship between the quantity of funds borrowed for investment purposes and the interest rate charged by lenders. That is, the Law of Demand applicable to this investment market states that *ceteris paribus,* as the rate of interest charged by lenders falls, the quantity of funds borrowed for purposes of economic investment increases.

---

[1] Hence, the flow of savings and investment is needed even in an economy that has neither a growing nor a declining circular flow.

Plausible reasons for the real world applicability of this law can be brought out by briefly describing the method whereby a "typical" borrower would determine the amount he would be willing to borrow at each possible interest rate. This will lay bare the economic variables determining the shape of the individual borrower's demand function, and since the market demand function is the sum of the individual demand functions, these same variables can plausibly [2] be said to determine the shape of the market function. For purposes of simplification we will assume the absence of risk.

The typical borrower will begin by listing the various projects in which he might invest. To each project he will assign an expected rate of return on the investment (net of all cost except interest on the borrowed funds). This will give him a table of potential investment projects such as those depicted by Table 3–1.

Having determined the investment opportunities, the typical investor will next determine the "price" of borrowing funds (i.e., the interest rate). He will then identify all potential investment projects yielding a return greater than the cost of borrowing funds, and he will borrow the funds needed to invest in these projects. For example, if the interest rate is 10 percent, the investor will discover (by turning to Table 3–1) that projects A, B, C, and D will return more than the cost of borrowing funds. Hence, he will want to borrow funds to invest in these four projects. Since these four projects involve a total investment of $10,000, our typical borrower will want to borrow $10,000.

Now, observe what happens as the interest rate falls. All the projects that were profitable at the higher rate are still profitable, and, in addition, new projects with lower yields become profitable. The result is that the total amount borrowed rises as the interest rate falls. For example, (returning to Table 3–1) if the interest rate were 10 percent our investor would borrow $10,000 to invest in projects A, B, C, and D. If the interest rate fell to 5 percent, $10,000 would still be borrowed for projects A, B, C, and D; and, in addition, another $15,000 would be borrowed in order to invest in projects E, F, G, H, I, and J. This raises total borrowing to $25,000. Thus,

---

[2] To argue that the behavior of the group is merely an aggregation of the behavior patterns of the individual members appears appropriate here. However, the student is reminded of the ever-present danger of committing the Fallacy of Composition. This fallacy consists of assuming that what is true of the individual members of a group will also be true of the group as a whole when in fact this is not so.

TABLE 3–1

Investment Demand

Project	Expected Rate of Return	Project Cost	Cumulative Cost
A	20%	$2,000	
B	15	3,500	
C	12	4,000	
D	11	500	
A,B,C,D			$10,000
E	9	1,500	
F	9	5,500	
G	8	1,000	
H	7	2,000	
I	6	2,000	
J	6	3,000	
E,F,G,H,I,J			$15,000
All Projects			$25,000

the slope of the individual and *market* demand curve for loanable funds can be explained in terms of the additional investment opportunities that the lower price (interest rate) of borrowed funds makes possible. The demand curve D_{LF} in Fig. 3–3 is an example.

Now, observe how the demand for loanable funds really reflects the borrowers' expectations concerning the future state of consumer demand. The funds are being borrowed for purposes of capital creation. The capital is being created in order to sell goods and services to consumers at some future date. Thus, the profits earned by the newly created capital will depend upon the future demand for the consumer goods produced by these capital goods. The return on investment is a measure of the market value that future consumers place on present investment.

The Supply of Noninflationary Loanable Funds

The source of noninflationary [3] loanable funds is saving. Saving can be undertaken by a variety of economic agents in a variety of

[3] The source of inflationary loanable funds is debt creation in the absence of a corresponding act of saving.

forms, but for purposes of simplification this chapter will assume that
only the households save.

Many factors influence the amount that a typical household will
save. One of these is "the interest rate." A plausible supply function
is presented in Fig. 3–3. Here we see a positive amount of saving

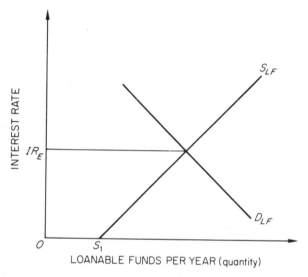

Fig. 3–3   The Market for Loanable Funds

(OS_1) at an interest rate of zero, indicating that factors other than
the interest rate induce saving. But we also note that as the interest
rate rises, the amount of saving also increases. Hence, we might
formulate a law of supply applicable to the loanable funds market,
which states, *ceteris paribus* (other things being equal), as the interest rate rises the supply of loanable funds (saving) also increases.

But why would households be willing to save more at a higher
rate of interest? The traditional answer has been that saving is a
means of giving up current purchases of consumer goods in order to
increase the amount of consumer goods that can be purchased in the
future. *Ceteris paribus,* the amount of future consumer goods that
can be purchased, will depend on the amount of savings and the
interest rate. As the interest rate rises, there is also an increase in the
amount of future consumer goods that a given amount of present
saving will purchase. Therefore, additional saving becomes more
"valuable" relative to current consumption.

An example may clarify the argument of the last paragraph. Suppose an individual has allocated all his current income with the exception of his last $10. He has narrowed his alternatives down to a choice between purchasing a $10 dress shirt and placing the $10 in a savings account earning 3 percent per year. At the end of one year, he could take the $10.00 plus interest (30 cents) out of the savings account and purchase the same dress shirt for $10. Thus, the choice is actually between a $10 dress shirt now and a $10 dress shirt plus 30 cents next year. Given this choice, our typical consumer buys the dress shirt. Now suppose that the interest rate has been 5 percent. In this case, saving the $10 for one year will provide 50 cents in addition to the shirt next year. The additional 2 percent (20 cents) may be sufficient to induce the individual to postpone the shirt purchase in the present. If not, surely, there will be some interest rate at which the individual will choose saving over some current purchases. This, is the assumption implicit in the slope of the supply curve of Fig. 3–3.

Partial Equilibrium Process

The demand and supply curves in the loanable funds "market" can be brought together, as in Fig. 3–4, to identify an equilibrium

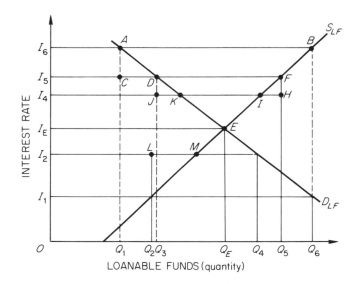

Fig. 3–4 The Loanable Funds Market

price (interest rate) and quantity. In this figure, the equilibrium rate of interest is OI_E. That this is a stable equilibrium can be readily demonstrated by identifying the dynamic equilibruim process, which tends to drive the interest rate toward OI_E. This equilibrium process differs from the Marshallian process. It can best be illustrated by considering interest rates above and below OI_E and observing what happens as time passes.

Let us begin with an interest rate above OI_E such as OI_6. At this rate of interest the loanable funds demanded (OQ_1) are less than the quantity of loanable funds supplied (OQ_6). Consequently, a portion of the supply of savings (loanable funds), the amount AB, cannot find interest paying borrowers. What will those who cannot find borrowers do? The traditional theory argued that some will withdraw their savings from the market altogether while others offer their savings at a rate below OI_6, such as OI_5.[4] At this lower rate additional borrowing also occurs in the amount CD.[5] This lower rate quickly becomes the market rate of interest as those savers who had been receiving the higher rate of interest find themselves forced to accept this lower rate if they are to avoid losing "customers."

But the interest rate of OI_5 still provides an excess of savings over the quantity demanded (OQ_3) of loanable funds, this amount being DF in Fig. 3–4. Therefore, some suppliers of loanable funds will again offer their savings at a lower price, and this will again drive the market rate of interest down to OI_4, causing the total volume of savings to again decrease by the amount HI while total borrowing increases by the amount JK.

Thus, starting at an arbitrarily chosen rate of interest that lies above the equilibrium rate, we have identified the first two steps in a dynamic process that moves the market rate of interest closer to the equilibrium rate of interest. Following the argument of the preceding paragraph, the student can easily construct the third, fourth, fifth, and additional steps, each of which would lead to a rate of interest below that prevailing at the end of the preceding step and each of which would bring the market rate of interest closer to the equilibrium rate. When will the process stop? Only when the market interest

---

[4] Unlike the Marshallian case, suppliers (savers) are assumed to be able to increase or decrease the quantity supplied immediately. That is, the long run becomes the short run, and the difference between the short run and very short run becomes analytically unimportant.

[5] As was the case in the Marshallian analysis, quantitative adjustments on the demand side occur immediately.

rate has fallen to that level where the entire quantity of loanable funds being supplied finds borrowers. There is only one such level of interest, and that is the equilibrium rate of interest, OI_E. Hence, the process we have just described is a process that drives the interest rate down to the equilibrium level.

Having identified a process that will drive the interest rate down to its equilibrium level whenever the market rate is temporarily above equilibrium, let us now consider the process that will drive a "low" interest rate up to the equilibrium level. Take any interest rate, such as OI_1, lying below equilibrium. At this rate, the quantity of loanable funds demanded, OQ_6, exceeds the quantity of savings supplied, OQ_2. What will those borrowers who cannot obtain loanable funds do? Some of them will offer to pay higher rates of interest such as OI_2. This will induce a net increase in saving (the amount LM). This will also reduce the quantity of loanable funds demanded from OQ_6 to OQ_4 because some borrowers will find some investment projects unprofitable at the higher rate of interest. Hence, the higher rate of interest increases saving, decreases borrowing, and brings the two closer together. But the market rate of interest, OI_2, is still below equilibrium, and, as a result, the quantity of funds demanded continues to exceed the amount supplied. Again, therefore, some borrowers offer to pay a higher rate of interest, and this causes saving to increase while the quantity of loanable funds demanded falls.

Thus, we have identified a process that drives the interest rate up toward equilibrium. At equilibrium the process will stop; for there will be no unsatisfied potential borrowers and, hence, no force tending to push the interest rate to a higher level. Since we have now identified one process that will push the interest rate down to the equilibrium rate whenever the market rate temporarily rises above equilibrium, and since we have identified another process that will always push rates below equilibrium up to equilibrium, we have established a *prima facie* case in support of the assertion that the intersection of the demand and supply functions in the loanable funds market is a position of stable equilibrium.

The partial equilibrium process just identified differs from the Marshallian process. This new process will be called the "bidding process." The basic difference lies in the absence of the time constraints that prevent the Marshallian process from working itself out before the long run. In the case of the bidding process, this time constraint disappears. The long run and the short run are identical, whereas the time period represented by the short run is sufficiently

short to make analytically meaningless the distinction between the
very short run and the short run.

Multimarket Partial Equilibrium:
Comparative Statics Analysis

In determining the rate of investment, the market process determines the portion of scarce resources that will be allocated to satis-
fying future wants. The preceding section discussed this proposition
using single market, partial equilibrium analysis. This section illustrates the same proposition with a comparative statics analysis of a
multimarket partial equilibrium model.

In order to simplify the discussion, let us assume that we have
an economy that produces two goods labeled the capital good and
the consumer good. Let us assume further that the production possibilities curve of Fig. 3–5 describes the present full capacity produc-

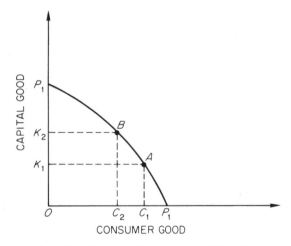

Fig. 3–5   Shifts of the Production Possibilities Curve

tion opportunities and that the demand and supply functions of Fig.
3–6 adequately reflect the state of the capital and consumer goods
markets. Finally, in Fig. 3–7, we find the demand and supply for
loanable funds.

Given these conditions, we can readily identify the initial equilibrium positions in each market and the resultant distribution of the

(a)

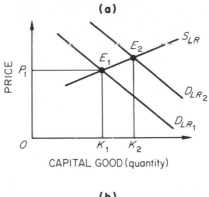

(b)

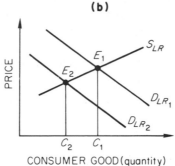

Fig. 3–6   Consumer-Capital Good Markets

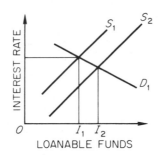

Fig. 3–7   Capital Good Market

economy's scarce resources between present consumption (consumer good) and future consumption (capital good). The market process yields an equilibrium output of OC_1 in the consumer good market and OK_1 in the capital good market. This is associated with position

A on the production possibilities curve. The demand for capital goods comes from those who borrowed funds for this purpose. Hence, the total amount borrowed (OI_1) in Fig. 3–7 is equal to the total amount spent in the capital good market $(OK_1 \cdot OP_1$ or the rectangle $OP_1E_1K_1$).[6]

The production possibilities curve focuses attention on the nature of the "sacrifice" that growth (capital formation) entails, for it shows us that the present level of capital good production is made possible only by foregoing consumer good production. Let us emphasize this point by referring to Fig. 3–5 and by assuming an increase in capital good production from OK_1 to OK_2 (that is, a movement along the production possibilities curve from A to B). This would occur if the demand curve for the consumer good shifted to D_{LR_2}, the demand curve for the capital good shifted to D_{LR_2}, and the supply curves for loanable funds shifted to S_2. Once these shifts have occurred, equilibrium forces [7] would establish new long-run equilibrium outputs of OC_2 in the consumer good market, OK_2 in the capital good market, and I_2 in the loanable funds market.

This is not the end of the process, for once the newly created capacity is utilized, the demand and supply curves in the capital good and consumer good markets will shift due to increased incomes and capacity. Furthermore, the increased income will cause the supply of savings schedule to shift to the right, and all these factors may cause a shift of the investment demand schedule. The shifts of the curves in the consumer and capital good markets will be discussed later in this chapter. The changes in the loanable funds market will not be discussed further since these are traditionally examined in macroeconomic analysis, and they are not essential for our purposes.

---

[6] This result follows only if we make one of two assumptions. First, we might assume that all "profit" and "depreciation" accruing to the sellers is returned to the households so that sellers must borrow from the households in order to obtain funds for the purpose of purchasing capital goods. Alternatively, we could assume that sellers retain depreciation funds and a portion of profits and use these to purchase capital equipment whenever the expected return on this investment is greater than any alternative investment and sufficiently high to induce the owners of the firm to forego the consumption expenditure that could have been made if these reinvested funds had been distributed to the owners (in their role as household members).

[7] Since we did not describe the adjustment process, this is not an example of dynamic analysis. As a matter of fact, the durable nature of capital goods and the volatility of investors' expectations raise serious questions with regard to both the adjustment process and the stability of the new equilibria.

MARKET DETERMINATION
OF THE RATE OF INNOVATION

In one way, the preceding discussion focuses upon the essence of the growth process by emphasizing the link between capital formation and increasing productive capacity. In another way, however, the preceding analysis is misleading, for the impression can easily be given that growth consists of additions to the total stock of capital when in reality much of the capital formation process may consist of replacing existing capital goods with new, more productive capital, so that the outward shift of the economy's production possibilities function is due to the adoption of more "efficient" production techniques. This process of institutionalizing new production techniques through the capital formation process is an example of the phenomenon called innovation.[8] It is a phenomenon that must be reckoned with if one is to understand the nature of economic growth and development.

The innovation process can be broken into two parts. First, there is the introduction of the new production technique by a single "firm." Economic thinking has attributed this act to the desire for monopoly profits. Discussion of this aspect of the innovation process will have to be omitted since the analysis of monopoly is not undertaken in sufficient detail in this text. Second, there is the attempt by other firms to tap the profitable market revealed by the successful innovation. This process is similar to the entry process discussed in Chapter 2, where the main difference usually lies in the fact that entry in the case of innovation would occur at a slower pace. In view of this similarity, we need not pursue the matter further now.

DETERMINATION
OF THE COMPOSITION OF GROWTH

The preceding discussion of the growth process is inadequate for our purposes due to its failure to point out how the newly created

---

[8] Actually the introduction of new production techniques represents only one of several forms of innovation. Others include the introduction of a new product, opening a new market, creating a new source of supply of inputs and carrying out a new organization. This categorization comes from Joseph Schumpeter, *The Theory of Economic Development* (Cambridge: Harvard University Press, 1949), p. 67.

productive capacity is allocated between the capital good and consumer good industries. In Fig. 3–8, for example, positions *B, C, D,* and *E* represent four different possible combinations of output once growth has increased the economy's capacity to P_2P_2. Position *B*

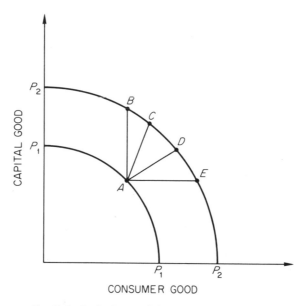

Fig. 3–8   Production Possibilities for Capital Good Use

represents the case where all the investment went to that portion of the capital good industry that produced "machines" to be used in the production of additional capital goods. Position *E*, on the other hand, is the case where all the investment went to that portion of the capital good industry that produces "machines" to be used to produce consumer goods. Position *C* represents the case where some of the investment was used to produce "machines" for capital good production and some investment has gone to produce machines for consumer good production. Position *D* represents a similar situation, but here the proportion of investment going into the expansion of consumer good capacity (producing "machines" that will be used to produce consumer goods) is greater than in the case represented by *C*.

How is the position on P_2P_2 selected? One method is through the market process. With the help of Fig. 3–9, let us trace out the steps in this particular market process. We begin with the system in

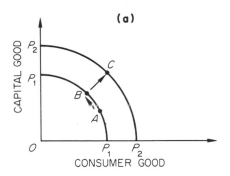

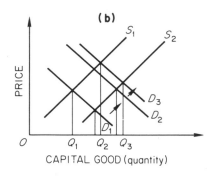

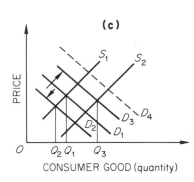

Fig. 3–9 The Market Selection of the Point on the *Production Possibilities Frontier*

static general equilibrium (position A on P_1P_1); assume a sudden "autonomous" shift of the demand curves in both the consumer and capital goods markets (from D_1 to D_2, in parts b and c); and observe the process evolve in the following sequence of events:

1. In the long run,[9] capital good production increases to OQ_2 while consumer good production decreases to OQ_2. These two changes are reflected by the movement on production possibilities curve P_1P_1 from A to B.

2. When the newly produced capital goods are put in place, the economy's productive capacity is increased. Therefore, the production possibilities curve shifts to P_2P_2.

3. As this newly created capacity is utilized, the newly created supply causes the supply curves to shift to S_2 in both markets. At the same time, the incomes created in the process of producing this supply cause the long-run demand curves to shift to D_3 in both markets.

4. These simultaneous shifts of the demand and supply curves cause

[9] The dynamic process leading to this long-run result would be the Marshallian process discussed in the previous chapter.

position C to be selected on the new production possibilities curve, with the output OQ_3 in both markets.

The market systems would immediately arrive at C only if producers *guessed correctly* as to how households would spend the additional income. If, instead, producers *expected* consumer demand to shift to D_4 and capital good demand to shift back to D_1, and if the demand curves actually shifted to D_3 in both markets, then producers in the consumer good market would find themselves incurring economic losses while producers in the capital good market would temporarily enjoy excess profits. In the absence of further growth, the reallocation process described in Chapter 2 would take place. Producers would leave the consumer good industry and enter the capital good industry, eventually pushing the economy to C on P_2P_2.

In either case, the market process selects the position on the production possibilities curve. But the possibility of misjudging the future state of demand alerts us to the need for a reconsideration of the role played by the producer-seller. Previously his role was presented in terms of reacting to a known demand. Now we have added the role of attempting to forecast demand. Demand is now considered to be uncertain. The producer-seller bears uncertainty [10] in guessing the future state of demand. If he overestimates the future state of demand, he will be forced to bear short-run losses. Hence, the analysis suggests that growth requires the existence of a producer group willing and able to bear this uncertainty in order for the market system to promote growth. As will be discussed later, the need for such a producer group has been the traditional argument in favor of allowing economic profits; that is, the function of profits is to encourage bearing uncertainty.

THE CONFLICT BETWEEN
RESOURCE ALLOCATION AND
PERSONAL SECURITY IN A GROWTH SETTING

The discussion of the preceding sections contains an interesting implication for the assertion made earlier that market systems are

[10] The layman often uses the word risk to describe this situation. However, risk and uncertainty have two distinct meanings in economic analysis. Risk refers to situations where the chance of an event occurring can be described by a known probability distribution. Uncertainty refers to the situation where such probabilities cannot be calculated.

plagued by a fundamental conflict between economic efficiency and personal security. Briefly stated, this implication is that in a growing economy resource reallocation may occur without any producers being forced to exit from their industry.

Exit Due to Need to Reallocate

Fig. 3–10 presents several possible growth paths to illustrate this point. Here, growth is portrayed by the production possibilities curve shifting outward from P_1P_1 to P_2P_2 to P_3P_3. Now, if the com-

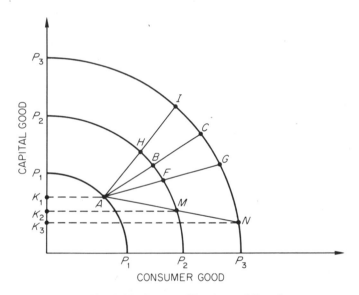

Fig. 3–10   Resource Allocation and Growth

binations of consumer and capital goods actually produced follow the path A to B to C, both industries expand production; and assuming that new techniques of production have not been devised, this expansion would allow all firms to remain in their original industry. There would be no exit from any industry as a result of economic losses. There would, however, be an increase in the proportion of the economy's resources devoted to consumer good production. In this sense, resource reallocation has occurred. Other expansion paths in Fig. 3–10 have this same property. For example, the paths A to H to I and A to F to G both involve an increased production of all goods. Hence, the growth process and the concomitant allocation of resources may occur without producing the personal insecurity previously encountered. There are, however, some growth paths in Fig. 3–10, which do involve the concomitant increase in personal insecurity. The path A to M to N is an example. In this case, growth from A to M leads to a decrease in the production of capital from OK_1 to OK_2. And further growth from M to N causes capital production to fall further to OK_3. This reduction in capital good production will be brought about by the exit of firms. The exiting firms will then enter the consumer good industry, completing the resource reallocation process "requested" by the market.

Exit Due to "Poor Guess"

It is also likely that growth will reduce the personal insecurity associated with the producer's "guess" as to the state of future demand. Earlier, it was argued that when entrepreneurs overestimated the state of demand in one market they would incur losses until some of them exited and entered the other market. Assume, for example, that in Fig. 3–11 the actual market demands call for producing at B when growth causes the PPC to shift to P_2P_2. Assume further that producers guessed incorrectly and installed capacity to produce at D. In the absence of further growth, this error would force some producers to exit from consumer good production and commence the production of capital goods. This process would continue until B had been reached.

If, however, growth continued, pushing the production possibilities curve to P_3P_3 with demand picking point E, exit might not have to occur, for the output of the consumer good that E represents would require more consumer good production capacity than that represented by D. Hence, if entrepreneurs could wait for growth to expand demand, they would be able to utilize the excess capacity created by the poor guess, which D represents. In such a case, the chances of personal insecurity occurring might be lessened.

Innovation and Personal Insecurity

The preceding examples assumed no technological change. Now, let us introduce a familiar type of technological change that, when

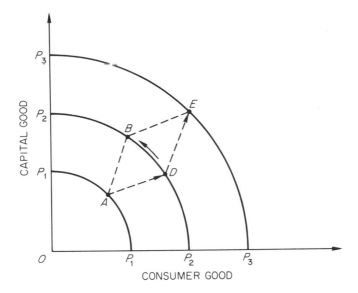

Fig. 3–11   Growth and Security

combined with slowly expanding demand, creates serious problems of personal insecurity.

Fig. 3–12 presents the basic model in diagrammatic form. In this model economy, there are two kinds of goods—an industrial good and an agricultural good. Growth is evidenced by the outward shift of the production possibilities curve from P_1P_1 to P_3P_3. The shifting demand and supply curves presented in parts b and c select the actual production points on the *PPC,* these being *A, B,* and *C.* In the case of the industrial good, the increasing output is accompanied by rising prices (P_1 to P_2 to P_3 in Fig. 3–12b. But notice what is happening to the price of the agricultural good. It is falling as growth takes place. How could this occur? One realistic possibility would be that technological change has drastically increased resource productivity, thereby causing the supply curve to shift rapidly to the right. If the demand curve fails to shift equally rapidly to the right, the price will fall. This has occurred in Fig. 3–12c where the price has fallen from P_1 to P_2 to P_3.

The falling price makes it impossible for those using the *old* production techniques to cover all their costs. (The role of the firm's cost function cannot be adequately discussed until cost curves have been developed. This analytical tool is not developed in the present text but can be found in any intermediate microeconomic theory text.) Therefore, the firms must either adopt the new techniques or

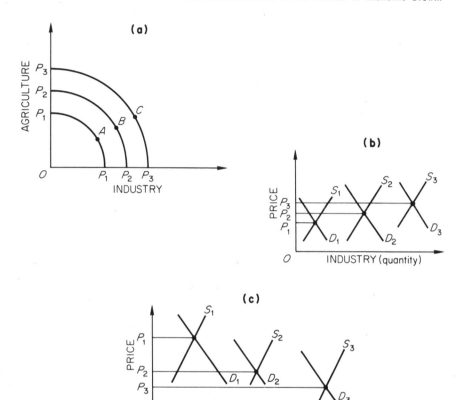

Fig. 3–12 Technological Change and Insecurity

leave the industry. If, as is often the case, the new techniques require a larger size of firm than was previously the case, some of the existing firms will have to leave the industry.

Such a process of new techniques leading to lower costs and forcing larger numbers of firms to exit is strikingly illustrated by the experience of American agriculture during the last thirty years. There is, of course, much more involved in America's agricultural problem than these crude tools reveal. Yet, in some ways, the model of Fig. 3–12 bares the essence of the so-called farm problem.[11] The

---

[11] The so-called farm problem is two problems, the exit problem described here and the problem of short-run instability of prices and income. Many observers add a third problem, poverty, but this is actually the result of the first two problems.

"problem" is the conflict between two goals of society: economic growth and personal security.

SUMMARY

Every economy must determine the proportion of its scarce resources that will be devoted to economic growth. Competitive market systems make this decision in the process of establishing equilibrium in the loanable funds market. Market systems also determine the composition of growth in the process of establishing equilibrium in the various product markets.[12] An important part of the growth process is the phenomenon of innovation. In the absence of innovation, the process of growth often enables resource reallocation to occur without forcing producers to exit from their original industry. However, when innovation is present, exit may be necessary. Hence, on occasion growth can conflict with the goal of personal security.

[12] For the sake of completeness, factor markets should also be included. This will be discussed in the next chapter.

4

The
Market
Solution
to the
Problem
of Income
Distribution

One of the earliest problems to be tackled by economists was that of the distribution of goods and services produced by the economy. Whereas the founder of the discipline, Adam Smith, regarded *the* problem of economic analysis as being the problem of growth, Smith's fellow classical economist David Ricardo believed that *the* task of the fledgling social science was to lay bare the forces determining the distribution of the economy's production. As he expressed it:

> The produce of the earth—all that is derived from its surface by the united application of labour, machinery and capital, is divided among three classes of the community . . . the proprietor of the land, the owner of the stock of capital necessary for its cultivation, and the labourers by whose industry it is cultivated. . . . [T]o determine the laws which regulate this distribution is the principal problem in political economy.[1]

Since the quantity of goods and services an individual receives depends essentially upon the money income he earns, this problem can be called the income distribution problem.

The income that an individual earns depends upon the amount of "property" he owns and the price of the "services" of his property. Supply and demand analysis is useful in explaining how the prices of the services are determined, but such market analysis does not do

---

[1] David Ricardo, *The Principles of Political Economy, and Taxation* (Homewood, Ill.: Richard D. Irwin, 1963), p. v. Ricardo's emphasis was upon income distribution in a growth setting.

a good job of explaining the distribution of property. So, as was the case in our discussion of the problem of growth, the market solution to the income distribution problem will not tell the entire story.

In discussing the role of the market process in the determination of an economy's pattern of income distribution, we will explore two aspects of the distribution issue. First, there is the distribution of income among each of the four groups of factors of production: labor, capital, land, and entrepreneurship in a stationary (nongrowing) economy. Second, there is the distribution among individual consumers, the individual owners of business "firms" and other types of individuals. Not discussed in this chapter is the distribution of income among the four factors of production in a growing economy.

ALLOCATION OF AND DISTRIBUTION AMONG FACTORS OF PRODUCTION IN A NONGROWTH SETTING

Let us begin by analyzing the impact of the competitive market system on income distribution in an economy that is not growing but is maintaining its current level of productive capacity. The market process affects income distribution by determining the price of each factor of production. In the case of labor, the price is called a "wage"; in the case of capital, the price is called "interest"; in the case of "land," the price is called "rent"; and in the case of entrepreneurship, there is no price but there is an occasional return, which is called profit. The present section considers the manner in which the market process determines these prices and uses them to distribute each factor of production among various competing uses.

Construction of the Derived Demand Function

Since this chapter uses market demand functions, a brief discussion of the nature of these functions might prove helpful. Market demand is the sum of the demands for labor by the various employers; therefore, the logical starting place is the demand function of the individual employer.

In determining the quantity of labor to be hired, the individual employing firm needs two pieces of information—the wage that must be paid and the revenue that the worker will earn for the firm. The wage to be paid is determined by the interaction of market demand for and supply of the labor. Since he represents a small portion of total market demand and hires a minute part of the total labor services purchased in the market, the individual employer takes the market determined wage as given. The manner in which the market determines this wage is discussed below.

In deciding what revenue will be provided by various amounts of labor input, the employer must determine:

1. The quantity of product output that the labor will produce;
2. The price at which this output will sell; and
3. The additional costs, exclusive of labor costs, which increased output involves.

Table 4–1 indicates the manner in which the employer might obtain this derived revenue function. First, the employer would obtain the information summarized in columns B and C. That is, he would estimate the total daily output of various amounts of labor; and, with this information at his disposal, he would calculate the change in physical output accruing to each additional unit of labor input. For example, knowing that three men each working an eight-hour shift will produce fifty-four television sets, and knowing that four men will produce sixty-nine sets, the employer calculates that employment of the fourth man will cause output to rise by fifteen sets per eight-hour shift. This fourth man's labor is called the marginal labor input, and the change in total physical output that it occasions is called the marginal physical product.

The marginal physical product associated with each additional man is shown in column C of Table 4–1. Notice that the marginal physical product falls as the number of men increases. Indeed, if the number of men employed rises to ten, the tenth man causes *no* change in total output.

The employer's second step is to determine the price at which the output will be sold. Since the employer sells his product in purely competitive markets, this price will remain constant regardless of the volume of sales. In this case, it has been assumed that this price is $100 per television set.

Having determined the price at which the product will be sold, the employer then multiplies the marginal physical product of each worker by the product price to obtain an estimate of the gross addition

TABLE 4–1

Calculations of Derived Demand Curve by Firm

(A) Labor Quantity of Input (number of man-days) [1]	(B) Total Physical Output of Producer of Televisions (number of sets)	(C) Marginal Physical Output of Last Input (number of sets)	(D) Price Per Unit of Output	(E) Gross Derived Marginal Revenue	(F) Associated Marginal Costs of Production and Distribution	(G) NET Derived Marginal Revenue
1	20	20	$100	$2,000	$200	$1,800
2	38	18	$100	$1,800	$200	$1,600
3	54	16	$100	$1,600	$200	$1,400
4	69	15	$100	$1,500	$200	$1,300
5	83	14	$100	$1,400	$200	$1,200
6	93	10	$100	$1,000	$200	$ 800
7	101	8	$100	$ 800	$200	$ 600
8	106	5	$100	$ 500	$200	$ 300
9	108	2	$100	$ 200	$200	$ 0
10	108	0	$100	$ 0	$200	$ −200

[1] Each man working 8 hours per day.

to revenue to be derived from the employment of that worker. For example, the fourth worker causes total revenue to rise by $1,500 since he causes total physical output to increase by fifteen units and each unit sells for $100. Since this increase in total derived revenue accrues to the marginal labor input, it is called the gross derived marginal revenue.

The revenue figures in column E are called gross derived marginal revenue because the employment of the marginal worker may entail expenditures for other, cooperating factors of production.[2] Hence, the costs of these factors must be deducted from the sums in column E in order to determine the change in total revenue accruing to the additional labor. Column F presents the marginal costs of cooperating factors of production associated with various marginal labor inputs. For example, the fourth man causes total revenue to rise by $1,500, but the increased output causes the cost of materials, tools, and other cooperating inputs to rise by $200. Hence the net increase in total revenue is $1,300 (1500 − 200 = 1300). It should be emphasized that this net derived marginal revenue represents the change in total revenue after all costs have been deducted *except* the cost of labor. Column G indicates the net revenue associated with each additional labor input.

The net derived marginal revenue represents the maximum wage that the employer could pay. That is, if three men were employed, the employer could pay each of them a wage of $1,400. If four men were employed, each could receive a wage of $1,300; and if five men were employed, the wage could be $1,200. This information is summarized in Fig. 4–1 where the curve D_1 shows the net derived marginal revenue associated with various additional labor inputs. In the long run, the wage paid by the employer is equal not only to the net derived marginal revenue but also to the net derived average revenue. Since the net derived average revenue is the maximum wage that the employer can pay without incurring losses, it can be said that in the long run no excess profit is earned.

The market demand curve for labor is merely the horizontal summation of individual firm curves such as D_1. It is inversely related to the wage rate because the demand curves of the individual firms

---

[2] It is common to assume that the other factors are fixed in amount so that there are no additional expenditures for other factors of production. However, the authors have chosen to follow the approach suggested by Joan Robinson, *The Economics of Imperfect Competition* (London: The Macmillan Company, Ltd., 1948).

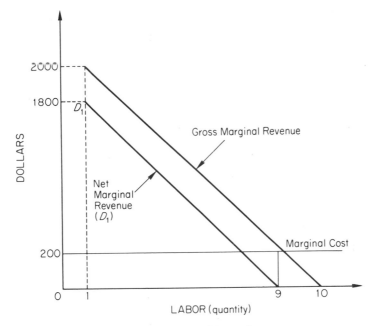

Fig. 4–1   Derived Demand

are inversely related to the wage rate. In the long run, the market demand curve represents the maximum wage that the employers can afford to pay without incurring losses, because this is what the individual firm curves represent in the long run.

Wages

Using the concept of derived demand, let us now explore the manner in which the competitive market process determines the level of wages and distributes labor services among alternative uses.

LEVEL OF WAGES.   First, let us look at the forces working to establish the general level of wages. This is best done by assuming the existence of a single market in which all the demand for labor services on the part of all "employers" confronts the economy's entire supply of labor.[3] Such a situation is portrayed by Fig. 4–2.

In the economy-wide labor market represented by Fig. 4–2, the

---

[3] The basic assumption is that each unit of labor is a perfect substitute for every other unit in all possible uses at all possible places in the economy.

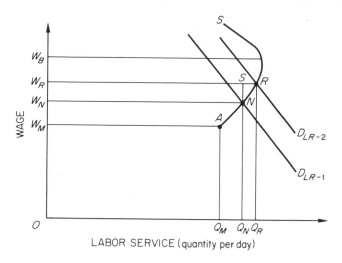

Fig. 4-2   Labor Market

demand for labor services shows the familiar negative slope, resulting from the assumption that employers will hire more labor at a lower money wage. The supply curve starts at a minimum wage, W_M, and extends horizontally to A where it begins to slope upward. The horizontal portion is obtained by assuming that OW_M is a subsistence wage, which must be paid if labor is to "survive," and that OQ_MAW_M is the total amount of wage income that the labor force would have to earn at this minimum wage in order to earn a subsistence income.[4] Thus, the horizontal portion of the supply curve indicates that the existing labor force will provide labor services at the subsistence wage of OW_M up to the amount of OQ_M. Beyond this amount, since the additional income is not needed for "subsistence"; since additional work means less leisure for the worker; and since leisure now becomes more valuable than the subsistence wage, employers must offer higher wages in order to induce laborers to give up more leisure. This results in the portion of the supply curve reflecting a direct relationship (quantity supplied rises with the rising wage rate). Should the wage rate rise beyond OW_B, the quantity of labor supplied will decline as workers begin to substitute leisure for hours worked. The

---

[4] This is extremely difficult to define in operational terms. A crude definition sufficient for purposes of the present discussion is that the minimum wage is that wage that will provide the worker with a money income just sufficient to allow him and the nonworking members of his family to maintain their existing standard of living.

higher wage allows labor to do this without sacrificing the previously achieved level of income.

Thus, as the wage rate rises above the subsistence level, the equilibrium process strikes a balance between the value of the leisure that labor gives up and the value of the income that labor receives. If long-run demand increases (shift from D_{LR_1} to D_{LR_2}), the wage rate rises in order to induce workers to give up additional leisure and spend the newly released time in production efforts. But since competition among employers brings about a common wage rate for all units of labor service, the higher wage rate that is paid in order to induce workers to give up leisure also becomes the wage rate paid for the labor services that would have been forthcoming at the subsistence wage. In Fig. 4–2, for example, a rise in the wage rate from W_N to W_R causes the quantity of labor to increase from OQ_N to OQ_R, and additional wages in the amount $W_N NRW_R$ are earned. This additional payment is a form of what is called economic rent. The old quantity of labor, OQ_N, receives rent of the amount $W_N NSW_R$; and, in addition to this rent payment, all the units of labor service added after OQ_N receive a rental return, with the exception of the very last unit. These payments are represented by the area NSR and will be explained later.

DISTRIBUTION OF LABOR SERVICES AMONG ALTERNATIVE EMPLOYMENTS.   The market processes working together determine the level of wages. Assuming each unit of labor to be a perfect substitute for every other unit; assuming perfect labor mobility; and assuming the sacrifice involved in every employment to be identical, the level of wages will be the same for all employments. However, the quantity of labor services allotted to each employment will not necessarily be identical. This allotment is determined by market forces, which we will now examine.

Partial equilibrium—Single market.   The supply and demand analysis developed earlier lends itself nicely to the study of the labor allocation process. To employ this analysis, we must drop the earlier technique of aggregating all demand into a single economy-wide demand function. Instead, we will now divide demand into two separate components—demand for labor on the part of consumer good producers and demand for labor on the part of capital good manufacturers. These two separate demand functions can be thought of as encountering the supply of labor services in separate markets. That is, it is assumed that there exist two markets for labor services, one where the consumer good industry purchases its labor and a second where the capital good industry hires its labor.

Fig. 4–3a depicts the market in which labor is hired by consumer good manufacturers. The curve D_{LR_1} represents the wage that consumer good producers are willing to pay for various quantities of labor services, the negative slope being a reflection of the factors considered in our earlier discussion of derived demand. The curve S_{LR} represents the quantity of labor services that workers will offer at various wage rates, *ceteris paribus*. This curve is horizontal, up to OQ_N, reflecting the fact that the determination of the wage level and the total quantity of labor services supplied to the economy are determined by all markets together, any one market being powerless to change either of these variables.[5]

D_{LR_1} and S_{LR} intersect at E_1, producing an equilibrium wage of W_1 and quantity of OQ_1. To indicate the stable nature of this labor market equilibrium, let us briefly describe the dynamic adjustment process portrayed by Fig. 4–3b. Starting at the initial equilibrium position E_1, the demand curve shifts to D_{LR_2}. In the very short run, no additional labor can be offered, so competing employers continue to hire OQ_1 labor and earn quasi-rents equal to W_1E_1AB. As time passes, some additional labor is hired so that by the end of the first week, output has increased and quasi-rents have been reduced to W_1SRT. Note that the one-week supply curve is perpendicular to the quantity axis, indicating that even after one week the quantity of labor supplied would not be responsive to price changes. In the long run, the increased supply of labor will push the quantity of labor services hired to OQ_2, and the quasi-rents will be eliminated altogether. Note that the wage remained at OW_1 throughout the entire adjustment process. Why this might occur is the subject of the following two sections.

Partial equilibrium—Multimarket analysis assuming fixed wages. Additional insight into the mechanisms at work is provided by a multimarket partial equilibrium analysis. Let us continue to consider the hypothetical economy in which only two goods are produced, these being a consumer good and a capital good.

---

[5] This assumption actually requires a large number of markets, the quantity of labor services purchased on any one of these being so small relative to the total labor supplied to the economy, that changes in the quantity hired in this one market would have imperceptible effects on the wage level.

(a) MARKET IN WHICH LABOR IS HIRED FOR EMPLOYMENT IN THE CONSUMER GOOD INDUSTRY – STATIC EQUILIBRIUM

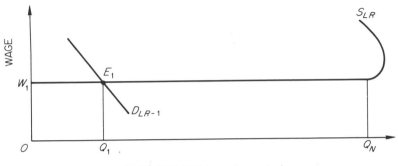

(b) SAME MARKET SHOWING DYNAMIC ADJUSTMENT PROCESS

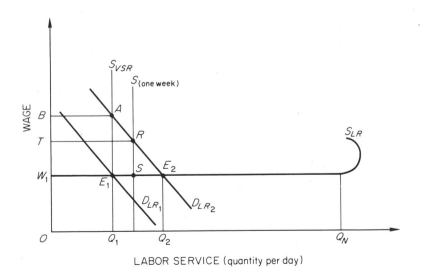

Fig. 4–3 Labor Market for Consumer Good Producers

Since these two commodities are produced by firms that buy their labor in separate markets, our model involves the four markets schematically presented in Fig. 4–4. Here we find the markets in an initial, mutually consistent set of equilibrium positions labeled E_1. Together, these positions put the economy at a position A on the production possibilities curve (note that in this chapter we are using a constant cost production possibilities curve).

Starting with this initial multimarket static equilibrium situation, let us now assume that the demand in the market system signals a need to reallocate resources in such a way as to move production to position B. This would be accomplished by the following shifts of the long run demand curves:

1. In the capital good market: (Fig. 4–4a) from D_1 to D_2, giving the new long-run equilibrium position E_2.
2. In the consumer good market: (Fig. 4–4b) from D_1 to D_2, producing the new long-run equilibrium position E_2.
3. In the labor for capital good production market: (Fig. 4–4c) from D_1 to D_2 giving the new long-run equilibrium position E_2.
4. In the labor for consumer good production market: (Fig. 4–4d) from D_1 to D_2 giving new long-run equilibrium position E_2.

But what dynamic process would insure the reallocation of resources as indicated by these shifts in demand? One answer is to be found in the mechanism described in Chapter 2. That is, starting with the initial shifts in the four demand curves, the following sequence of events would take place:

1. In the very short run, only prices and wages can be altered; hence, in the capital good market purchasers quickly bid the very short-run price up to A and in the consumer good market, sellers quickly bid the price down to A.

In the market where labor services are hired for use in capital good production, long-run quantity demanded exceeds long-run quantity supplied; and since no quantity adjustment can be made in the very short run, it might be expected that the price of labor (the wage rate) would rise to ration the existing supply among competing employers. However, this will not occur because in the very short run there exists no labor that can move from one employer to another and hence there exists no opportunities for employers to bid wages up.

In the market where labor is hired for employment in the con-

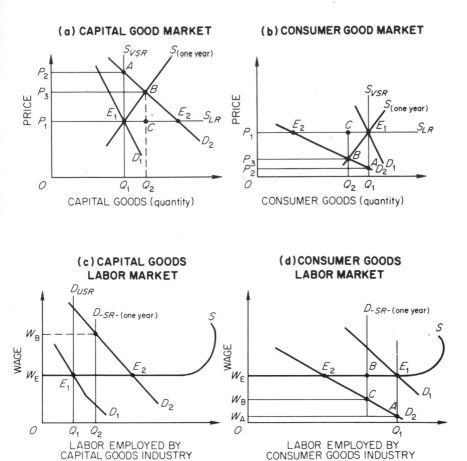

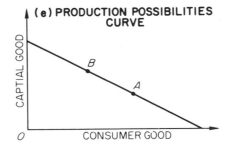

Fig. 4-4   Partial Equilibrium—Multimarkets for Goods and Labor

sumer good industry, it might be expected that wages would be bid down to W_A. However, since no labor services will be forthcoming at a wage rate below W_E, employers cannot lower wages. The only alternative is to reduce the quantity of labor services employed. But in the very short run, even this cannot be done, so the employers [6] must absorb economic losses amounting to $W_A A E_1 W_E$.

2. In the short run, some adjustments are possible. At the end of one year, for example, capital good production and the quantity of labor services hired by capital good producers have expanded while consumer good production and the quantity of labor services hired by consumer good producers has declined.

Capital good production has expanded to OQ_2, pushing the price down to OP_3 but still providing quasi-rents in the amount of P_3BCR. Consumer good production has fallen to OQ_2, and the price has risen. As a result, economic losses have been reduced but not eliminated (losses are now equal to the area P_3BCP_1).

In the two labor markets, the wage rate remains unchanged but there have been quantity adjustments. In the labor market where labor is hired by capital good producers, the quantity of labor services purchased has increased to OQ_2. It might be expected that competing employers would bid the price of these labor services up to W_B as suggested by the short-run demand curve $D_{SR\,1\,\text{year}}$. However, assuming that this would occur only if employers had unused capital that the additional labor could utilize and assuming that such unused capital does not exist, then there would be no reason for employers to bid against one another for the available labor. In the absence of such bidding, the wage rate would not rise.

At this point, a word on the curve $D_{SR\,1\,\text{year}}$ is in order. This short-run demand curve shows the quantity of labor demanded at the end of one year. It is drawn perpendicular to the quantity axis in order to reflect the assumption that the quantity of labor demanded in the short run is a function of the ability of the employers to expand

___

[6] In order to obtain this result it might be assumed that at the beginning of this very short-run period, employers were paid for the work to be done. Hence, wages in the amount $OQ_1E_1W_1$ have already been paid and will be lost regardless of whether or not production occurs. In this case, employers would want to minimize their loss by producing OQ_1 and selling this output to recover a portion of the wage bill. OQ_1AW_A would be recovered, leaving the employer with a loss of $W_A A E_1 W_E$. The alternative would be to produce less and incur greater net losses. The extreme case would occur if employers reduced output to zero. In this case, their net losses would rise to $OQ_1E_1W_A$. Alternatively, it could be assumed that the loss actually accrues to some other fixed factor of production.

capacity and this process of expanding capacity does not cause the wage rate to rise.

The short-run (one year) adjustment in the market where labor is hired for use in consumer good production releases the labor that was added by the capital good industry. The decline in labor services purchased by consumer good producers is indicated by the intersection of S and $D_{SR_{1 \text{ year}}}$. $D_{SR_{1 \text{ year}}}$ is a short-run demand curve representing the capacity adjustments made by the consumer good firms during the first year following the price decline. $D_{SR_{1 \text{ year}}}$ cuts the long-run demand curve, D_2, at C, indicating that losses are still being incurred in the amount of $W_E BC W_B$. Thus, consumer good production is not in long-run equilibrium, for much of the original capacity is still in place, and losses will continue to be incurred until the excess capacity has been completely eliminated in the long run.

It should be noted that the decline in employment in the consumer good industry need not occur at the same rate as the increase in employment in the capital good industry. Indeed, it is quite likely that the consumer good industry will release workers faster than the capital good industry will hire them. In this case, unemployment will temporarily rise. For the time being, it will be assumed that this labor does not offer itself at lower wages. An adjustment process in which the unemployed labor does offer itself at a lower wage is discussed in the next section.

3. In the long run, the capital good producers are able to add the additional productive capacity and hire the labor that was temporarily employed in the consumer good industry and thus arrive at equilibrium position E_2 (Fig. 3–4a); the consumer good market also arrives at its new long-run equilibrium position (E_2 in Fig. 3–4b); and the two labor markets arrive at their new long-run equilibrium positions (E_2 in Fig. 3–4c and 3–4d). In the process, the economy has moved from position A to position B on the production possibilities curve (Fig. 3–4e).

Partial equilibrium—A multimarket analysis assuming flexible wages. The dynamic adjustment process just described was based on the assumption that wage rate did not change. Such an assumption is not essential to the discussion of the way in which the market process allocates labor among industries. Indeed, the classical approach emphasized wage flexibility.[7] Furthermore, discussion of an

---

[7] This requires that wages be above subsistence levels.

adjustment process with flexible wages is essential in order to demonstrate the role of competition in bringing about equal wages in all
employments.

Fig. 4–5 presents the flexible wage model. In terms of comparative static analysis, this model is identical with that of Fig. 4–4.
That is, the demand curves in all markets shift from D_1 to D_2, and,
in the long run, these shifts result in the new equilibrium positions E_2.
What distinguishes the flexible wage case of Fig. 4–5 from Fig. 4–4
is the dynamic adjustment process, which evolves in the following
fashion:

1. In the very short run, only prices and wages can be altered.
Hence, in the capital good market the price of the product is bid up
to $A(OP_2)$ and in the consumer good market the price falls to
$A(OP_2)$.

In the market where labor services are hired for use in capital
good production, the wage of labor is quickly bid up to $A(OW_1)$.
This is done in spite of the fact that total industry output cannot be
increased. Why, then, would employers bid the wage up? One possible explanation is that the other factors of production are in sufficient
supply to allow increased output if additional labor can be hired. The
additional labor is not available to the industry as a whole, but
individual firms can increase their labor inputs by hiring labor services away from others. Hence, employers bid against one another
for the scarce labor, forcing the wage to rise.

In the market where labor is hired to work in consumer good
production, the wage is immediately bid down to $A(OW_1)$. This is
due to the fact that consumer good producers have laid off some
workers and these workers, unable to move to the other market in
the very short run, offer their services to the consumer good employers at lower wage rates. This process of offering to work for a
lower wage continues until the wage rate falls to W_1 where all labor
is employed.[8]

2. In the short run, some adjustments are possible. At the end
of one year, for example, capital good production and the quantity
of labor services hired by capital good producers have increased while
the reverse is true in the consumer good industry and its associated
labor market. The expansion of capital good production and con-

---

[8] Of course, at this lower wage rate, some of the labor may temporarily
retire from the labor force as suggested in Fig. 4–2. We will ignore this problem for the time being.

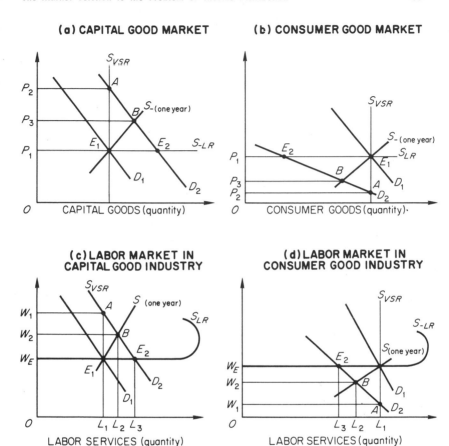

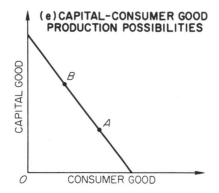

Fig. 4–5 Dynamic Adjustment Process with Wages Flexible

traction of consumer good production are identical to the one year changes described in Fig. 4–4. The expansion of the labor services used in capital good production is caused by labor leaving the low wage consumer good industry and coming to work in the higher wage capital good industry (curve $S_{1\text{ year}}$ reflects this). In order to obtain employment in the capital good industry, these workers must offer their services at a lower wage, and this forces the workers already employed in the capital good industry to offer their services at a lower wage in order to keep their jobs. Consequently, newly arrived workers and the original workers bid the wage down until there are jobs for all. This new, lower wage is W_2, which, while lower than W_1, is still higher than the wage paid in the other industry.

In the other labor market, the departure of some of the labor removes some of the pressure causing the wage rate to settle at W_1, and, as a result, the wage rises to W_2. W_2, of course, is determined by the intersection of the new long-run labor demand function (D_2) and the one-year labor supply curve ($S_{1\text{ year}}$). This new wage is still lower than that available in the capital good industry, so additional labor can be expected to leave the consumer good industry as additional time elapses.

3. In the long run, capital good output expands to E_2, and consumer good output declines E_2. In the labor market serving the capital good industry, employment has expanded to E_2, forcing the wage down to W_E; whereas in the labor market serving the consumer good industry, employment has fallen to E_2, causing the wage to rise to W_E.

Thus, wages have been equalized in the two employments as a result of workers in the lower paying industry moving to the higher paying industry. In the process, resources have been reallocated, causing a movement from A to B along the production possibilities curve.

The rather austere properties of the preceding dynamic process can easily be made more realistic by crossing this process with that of the previous section, producing a model in which wages are flexible but not so flexible as to eliminate quasi-rents in the very short run and short run. However, we will not attempt such a task in the remaining pages.

INCOME DISTRIBUTION AND WELFARE.   In the process of allocating labor among the various alternative uses, the market process determines the income that each laborer will receive for his services. Hence, in the absence of alternative sources of income, the market process determines the distribution of income within the economy.

What can be said about the desirability of this market-determined distribution? Unfortunately, the ultimate evaluation requires nonscientific judgments and therefore lies beyond the analytical reach of economics. There are, however, several properties of the market result that should influence the ultimate judgment and should therefore be noticed at this point.

First, it should be observed that the market process tends to equalize wages in all alternative uses. This is accomplished by the ability of labor in low paying employments to move to industries with higher wages. In practice, of course, barriers to such movements interfere with the wage equalization tendency. Such impediments as differences in job attractiveness, skills, and artificial restrictions on entry are examples of such barriers.

Second, labor's wage tends to be the maximum that employers can afford to pay without incurring losses. This proposition follows from the derivation of the derived demand curve, which was explained earlier in the chapter.

Third, the equilibrium wage tends to equalize the social benefits and social costs of employing labor in each particular use. This somewhat tautological statement assumes that the maximum wage that employers are willing to pay is a measure of the marginal social benefit accruing to the use of that labor, whereas the minimum wage that must be paid (given by the supply curve) is a measure of the marginal social cost of using the labor. Since optimal resource allocation requires that marginal social benefit equal marginal social cost and since this only occurs where the demand and supply curves cross, this equilibrium position must be socially optimal.[9]

Interest

THE LEVEL OF THE INTEREST RATE.   The preceding discussion on growth discussed the manner in which the demand for and supply of loanable funds determines the level of the interest rate. That discussion brought out the fact that such funds are the basis of capital formation and that beyond a certain minimum level of saving, the economy can only induce additional funds for capital formation

[9] Refer back to Chapter 2 for a discussion of this rule.

through the payment of a higher interest. Competition pushes the interest rate to a level where the demand and supply curves intersect (E_1 in Fig. 4–6). At this point, those supplying the loanable funds are receiving the minimum interest payment necessary to induce them to save this amount while this same amount is the maximum that the "last" borrower can afford to pay for the "last" loan.

But this amount is less than the maximum sum that many other borrowers could afford to pay and still make a "normal" profit. For example, those borrowing funds totalling OQ_2 in Fig. 4–6 could

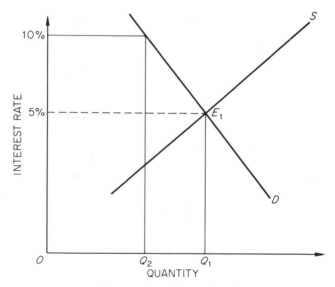

Fig. 4–6   Loanable Funds Market

afford to pay at least a 10 percent rate of interest. Hence, some savers are not receiving the total amount that borrowers could afford to pay and still cover all their costs including a normal profit.

Distribution of Loanable Funds Among Alternative Uses. Would this difference between what borrowers can afford to pay and what they actually pay be maintained? To answer this question we must look at the manner in which the competitive market process allocates capital funds (and therefore capital goods) among the various "industries" within the economy. Fig. 4–7 presents a diagrammatic statement of this model. As is readily apparent, Fig. 4–7 is identical with Fig. 4–4 except for the labels on the two axes. The

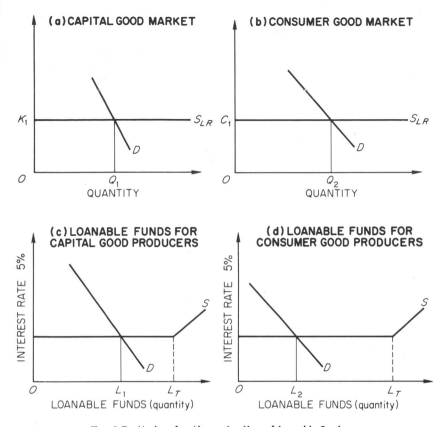

Fig. 4–7 Markets for Alternative Uses of Loanable Funds

horizontal axis measures the quantity of loanable funds instead of the quantity of labor services while the vertical axis measures the interest rate instead of the wage rate.

Let us briefly review the properties of static multimarket equilibrium in Fig. 4–7. In the final goods market, the capital good (Fig. 4–7a) and the consumer good market (Fig. 4–7b) both exhibit demand and supply curves with familiar slopes. These demand and supply functions produce long-run equilibrium prices of OK_1 and OC_1 and equilibrium quantities of Q_1 and Q_2. The two factor markets are: (1) the market for loanable funds to be used to purchase capital goods for later use in consumer good production; and (2) the market for loanable funds to be used to purchase capital goods for later use in the production of capital goods. The supply curves in both these markets have horizontal stretches beginning at the origin and extending to the amount of funds that savers are willing to supply to the economy as a whole at that rate of interest (5% in Fig. 4–7). As was the case in the labor market discussion, the demand curves in these two loanable funds markets are derived from the demand and supply conditions in the final goods markets.

The static equilibrium condition depicted by Fig. 4–7 immediately calls into question the earlier suggestion that some borrowers of loanable funds are using these funds to earn an amount exceeding the cost of the funds. This is so because the intersections of the long-run demand and supply functions in the final goods market show no sales revenue in excess of cost. Therefore, any excess earned on the borrowed funds could not have gone to the owners of the business firms who borrowed the funds.

What dynamic adjustment process assures us that the equilibrium situation depicted in Fig. 4–7 will, in fact, be reached? A process similar to that described in the flexible wage case seems appropriate. By substituting the word loanable funds for the word labor in Fig. 4–5c and 4–5d, we would have the basic process. This exercise will be left to the student.

WELFARE IMPLICATIONS OF THE MARKET PROCESS.[10] The preceding discussion suggests that a purely competitive market system would tend to squeeze excess profits out of the hands of the borrowers of loanable funds and into the hands of the suppliers of savings or into the hands of buyers in the form of lower product prices. Consequently, the interest paid for loanable funds tends to equal the net return earned on the capital by the borrower after deducting all costs (including a normal profit). At the same time, this rate tends to equal the average (and marginal) costs of supplying the saving. Hence, the market process tends to produce a level of capital formation that equates the marginal social benefits of the capital formation with its marginal social costs.

Rent

In the course of analyzing market determination of wages and interest, the earlier discussion revealed that labor and capital often received payments in excess of those needed to induce the corresponding supply of labor and capital services. These "excessive" payments are examples of the phenomenon that economists call economic rent.

---

[10] A discussion of interest equalization is not needed since the discussion of wage equalization makes the necessary points.

THE LEVEL OF RENT.   Let us briefly review this concept with the
aid of Fig. 4–8, which presents the economy-wide models of the labor
and capital markets. In the labor market, the wage level of OD, giving
the quantity OF of labor services, produces a labor income of $OFEB$.
Of this income the amount $OAEF$ is required to call forth the quantity
OF of labor services. But competition forces employers to pay the
additional amount ABE.[11] This additional amount is the economic
rent received by labor. Similarly, in the capital market interest in the
amount of $OABC$ is paid as a result of competition for the scarce
capital services. Of this amount, the sum DAB represents economic
rent, which the suppliers of capital receive as the result of competition
among borrowers.

The third market depicted in Fig. 4–8 is the economy-wide

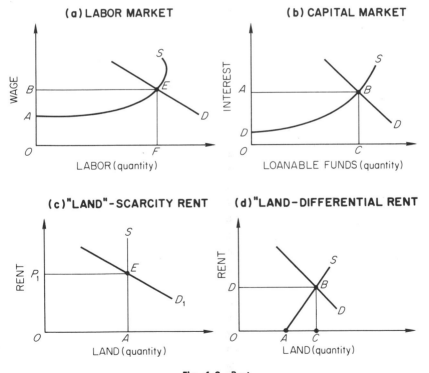

Fig. 4–8   Rent

[11] In the absence of competition among employers this surplus would
be captured by the employers. Similarly, in the absence of full employment as
defined above, this surplus would be shifted from labor to other factors of
production as discussed below.

market for "land." This is the market that economists usually turn to in order to illustrate the nature of economic rent. There are two distinct situations in the case of land. One assumes a supply curve to be perpendicular to the quantity axis at some positive quantity such as OA in Fig. 4–8c. Such a supply curve, called a perfectly price inelastic supply curve, indicates that the quantity of OA of "land" will be available to the economy as a whole regardless of price. Therefore, no price need be paid in order for the economy to obtain this "land."

But a price will be paid, because this "land" is limited in supply while its use will provide profits for those who use it. Hence, there is a demand as depicted by the curve D_1, and this demand, interacting with supply, establishes an equilibrium price, P_1. As a result, the quantity OA of land receives an income of $OAEP_1$. This income is an economic rent because none of the income is needed in order to induce this quantity of land into the market. This type of rent is called a scarcity rent.

The second type of rent generated in the land market is illustrated by Fig. 4–8d. The amount OA of land is available at a zero price, but beyond this the quantity of land supplied does increase as the price rises. For example, if the price rises from zero to OD, the quantity of land supplied rises by AC. And here, as was the case with loanable funds and labor services, the rising price, although necessary to induce an increase in the quantity supplied, is also responsible for the creation of rent (the amount $ODBA$ in Fig. 4–8d). This kind of rent is called differential rent.

DISTRIBUTION OF LAND AMONG ALTERNATIVE USES. Confining our attention to the case of scarcity rent, an interesting question arises. What is the economic function of this price if it is not needed to induce the supply of a factor of production to become economically active? The answer is to be found in the performance of the familiar task of allocating this scarce resource among the competing alternative uses. Let us briefly review this function by referring to the multimarket model of Fig. 4–9 which presents the markets in which the services of land are purchased for use in the production of the consumer good (Fig. 4–9d) and for the production of the capital good (Fig. 4–9e). In addition, we also find the markets for the consumer good (Fig. 4–9b) and the capital good (Fig. 4–9c) and the aggregate market for land (Fig. 4–9a).

Let us assume that these markets are initially in long-run competitive equilibrium at the positions indicated by E_1 in each market.

(a) AGGREGATE MARKET FOR LAND

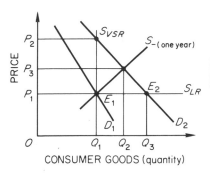

(b) CONSUMER GOOD MARKET

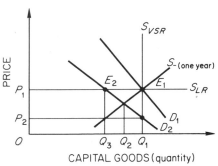

(c) CAPITAL GOOD MARKET

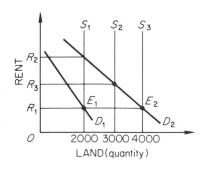

(d) "LAND" USED IN CONSUMER GOOD PRODUCTION

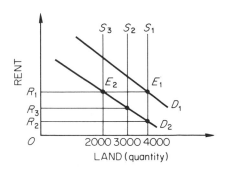

(e) "LAND" USED IN CAPITAL GOOD PRODUCTION

Fig. 4–9

Then, let us assume a shift in all demand curves from D_1 to D_2. This sets in motion the following dynamic adjustment process.

1. In the very short run, no supply adjustments can be made in the product markets but price adjustments can occur. Hence, as discussed earlier, the consumer good price rises to OP_2 while the capital good price falls to OP_2.

In the "land" markets, let us assume that all the quasi-rent and economic loss are transferred to the suppliers of land. Hence, the 2,000 units of land initially being supplied to the consumer good producers suddenly find their price rising to R_2. And the 4,000 units of land being supplied to the capital good producers suddenly find their price falling to R_2.[12]

2. In the short run, land receiving low rent from capital good producers is gradually moved into employment in the consumer good industry. At the end of one year, for example, 1,000 units of "land" have moved out of capital good production into consumer good production, causing the rental payment received by the land in the consumer good industry to fall to R_3, whereas the rent received by the land remaining in capital good production rises to R_3. These changes are shown by a shift of the short run supply curves from S_1 to S_2 in Fig. 4–9d and 4–9e.

In the product markets, the falling price of "land" available to consumer good producers causes consumer good production to expand to OQ_2, and the rising price of land available to capital good producers causes the quantity of capital good output to decrease to OQ_2.

3. In the long run, sufficient land has left the capital good industry to raise the rent received by the remaining land to R_1 The supply of land to each industry has changed as indicated by the S_3 supply curves in Fig. 4–9d and 4–9e. The land which has departed from the capital good industry has gone into consumer good employment where its arrival has pushed the rent of land back down to R_1. Thus, the rent received by land has been returned to its economy-wide level of R_1 in all uses. This has been accomplished by a process of redistributing land among its two alternative uses. The amount of land used in capital good production has declined from 4,000 to 2,000 units whereas the amount of land used in consumer good production

---

[12] In order to obtain this result, it will be assumed that the price of land is continually renegotiable within a market even though the equilibrating movements of units of land from one market to another can only be completed in the long run.

has increased from 2,000 to 4,000 units. The total amount of land in use remains at 6,000 units. Only its distribution has changed.

As a result of this distribution, the composition of final output has also changed. Consumer good production has risen to the level of output OQ_3 while capital good production has fallen from OQ_1 to OQ_3.

The preceding does not exhaust the list of possible adjustment processes. An alternative might maintain the rental rate at R_1 and cause land to be redistributed in a fashion analogous to that discussed in the case of the labor adjustment process with fixed wages. Similarly, various combinations of these two processes might be developed.

WELFARE IMPLICATIONS. The preceding suggests that economic rent must be paid if the competitive price system is to force land into its socially most desirable uses. As was the case with labor and capital, the price paid for the use of land is a payment needed to distribute "land" among alternative uses in such a manner as to maximize social benefits and minimize social opportunity costs.

In passing we might note that the necessity of paying rent does not mean that the original recipients of the rent must be allowed to retain all this surplus income. The government may be able to tax the surplus away. If this occurs, the act of taxation will not affect the supply of factors of production. Hence, to the extent that the objective of taxation is to raise revenue with a minimum of interference in private productive activity, the identification of rents becomes an important part of tax policy.

Profits

The fourth payment to factors of production is economic profit. This is defined as the payment that "entrepreneurs" receive for bearing uncertainty. Therefore, the economist's definition of profit is narrower than the definition implicit in everyday conversation, for the noneconomist is prone to include rent, interest, and wages in the implicit definition of profits. The determination of profits is not brought about by simple market processes such as those determining rent, wages, and interest. Consequently, a somewhat different analytical framework is required, but it will not be developed in this text.

The preceding gave an impressionistic picture of the role of the market process in determining the distribution of income among factors of production in a stationary (nongrowing) economy. It was shown that the market process determines prices of capital and labor, which have some claim to being "fair" prices at the margin [13] and which have a strong claim to being efficient at the margin. It was also shown that rental incomes may be earned by intramarginal units of "land," labor, and capital; and, at least in the case of "land," it was suggested that these rental incomes might "fairly" be captured through taxation without interfering with the allocative function of the prices that produced the rent.

The approach in the preceding pages was a multimarket partial equilibrium approach. This avoided certain problems that a general equilibrium analysis must confront. One of these has to do with the effect of changing income distributions on demand functions in the product markets and the supply of saving function in the loanable funds market. Another has to do with reconciling the dynamic adjustment processes in the factor markets when it is assumed that factor prices are flexible.

DISTRIBUTION AMONG
CONSUMERS, FIRM OWNERS, AND
OTHER FACTORS OF PRODUCTION

The discussion of the payment of factors of production represents one method of approaching the income distribution implication of the competitive market system. An alternative method of looking at the income distribution implications of such a system is to divide recipients into three groups: consumers, employers, and factors of production. Having done this, we can then investigate the impact of the competitive market process on the "income" received by each of these groups.

Fig. 4–10 presents a diagrammatic summary of the income distribution effects. The market represented by Fig. 4–10 contains business "firms" offering the product for sale and households offering to

---

[13] The last unit of the factor employed receives an income no larger and no smaller than a "fair" income. Clearly, the judgment that these prices are fair is a value judgment. What the preceding pages have presented is the basis of such a judgment. It should also be noted that labor bears the major burden of the competitive adjustment process through potential wage or employment loss and that this risk or uncertainty would clearly need to be taken into account when making value judgments with respect to wages.

purchase the product. The business "firms" hire the services of land, labor, and capital in factor markets (not shown in Fig. 4–10) and use these services to produce the product. The supply curve shows the cost of these factors of productions per unit of product output. For example, in order to supply the amount OQ_1 of the product, the business firms have to hire an amount of land, labor, and capital,

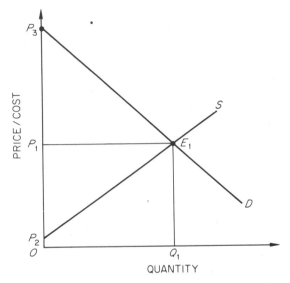

Fig. 4–10   The Product Market-Rent and Consumer Surplus

which costs OP_1 for each of the OQ_1 units. Another way of expressing this is to say that the production of OQ_1 units of the product requires the payment of $OQ_1E_1P_1$ to the factors of production in the form of wages, rent, and interest. Of this payment, the portion $P_1E_1P_2$ represents rent accruing to the various factors of production.

   On the demand side there also exists a phenomenon similar to rent. This is the area $P_3E_1P_1$. This area represents the amount by which consumer valuation of the quantity OQ_1 exceeds the amount that purchasers must pay sellers in order to acquire the item. This area could be called consumer rent, reflecting the fact it is a surplus amount of "value," which consumers receive in excess of the price that is paid. However, economists do not call this consumer rent. Instead the literature refers to this as consumer's surplus.[14]

   [14] The concept of consumer surplus is far more complex than the preceding passage implies. But for the purposes of the present text, what has been said is sufficient.

The income distribution implications of the competitive market process should now be apparent. The process discriminates against the owners of business firms in the sense of forcing rent-like surpluses out of the hands of these owners and into the hands of other factors of production and consumers. Since the individuals who own the firms are also consumers, they do benefit from the process in their consumer capacity; and since the individuals who own the firms may also supply labor services and receive a rent-like payment for these, it cannot be said that the owners suffer a net loss of income as a result of the process. But it can be said that the competitive market system has an income distribution mechanism that is biased against the business firm. That is, the business-oriented economy is in fact biased against business.

SUMMARY

This by no means exhausts the income distribution implications of the competitive market process. For example, Ricardo, whose authority was invoked at the beginning of this chapter, was fundamentally concerned with the effect of economic growth upon the distribution of national income among wages, rent, and "profit." Yet this topic has not been mentioned in the preceding pages, and it will not be considered in the remainder of the text.[15] Nevertheless, what has been covered in the preceding pages is sufficient to indicate the nature of the market solution to the social problem of income distribution. It is a solution that has some claim to "fairness" insofar as wages and interest are concerned, but it undeniably produces rental incomes that are likely to be adjudged socially "unfair." Fairness aside, the market solution also has some claim to producing efficient results, even in the process of producing rental incomes. Here again we see the fundamental phenomenon of conflicting objectives.

[15] In addition to Ricardo's *Principles* cited above, the student might consult the literature on economic development for several descriptions of the Ricardian dynamic analysis. See, for example, Robert Baldwin and Gerald Meier, *Economic Development: Theory, History, Policy* (New York: John Wiley and Sons, 1957), pp. 25–44.

5

The

Market

Solution

to the

Problem

of Economic

Instability

E conomic efficiency, economic growth, personal security, and a desirable allocation of factor payments do not exhaust the list of performance norms. Equally important is the goal of economic stability. Traditionally, stability refers to prices and employment. In terms of prices, the most pressing problem is likely to be "inflation," while in terms of employment the problems consist of "cyclical and structural unemployment." Both these problems are customarily discussed in the literature of macroeconomic analysis. But microeconomic analysis can provide some insight into the forces at work. Indeed, at one time microeconomic analysis was used by economists to prove the impossibility of unemployment. The present chapter reviews the traditional arguments with respect to unemployment.[1] Customarily linked with the stability problem has been yet another problem, that of balance-of-payments equilibrium. This problem is also discussed in the present chapter.

UNEMPLOYMENT

Unemployment may be said to exist when some suppliers of labor services who are willing and able to work at the prevailing wage rate are unable to find jobs. The traditional analysis of such unemployment led to the conclusion that whereas temporary or short-run un-

[1] Since most of what follows is usually handled by courses in macroeconomic analysis, the main justification for including the material here is to give the student a better understanding of the argument that the competitive price system is an all-purpose decision system.

employment was a healthy and necessary part of the competitive adjustment process, permanent or long-run unemployment was made impossible by the equilibrium processes at work in the labor and capital markets. Let us briefly review this argument.

Existence of Temporary Unemployment

The argument that temporary unemployment is an important ingredient of the competitive market adjustment process was discussed in the preceding chapter. The discussion of Fig. 4–3 revealed the fact that, in the process of reallocating resources, the market temporarily forced labor out of employment in one industry in order to enable this labor to be employed elsewhere. This discussion suggested that as soon as workers leave one industry, they are immediately employed by the other. In fact, since there are many employers, some of whom desire additional labor and some of whom do not, the laborers leaving one industry may have to "search" for those industries where the available jobs are to be found. During the time that passes while the laborers search for these new jobs, they are unemployed. But this unemployment is temporary. The jobs are waiting and will eventually be found. Furthermore, the unemployment serves the useful purpose of goading the workers into searching for these new job opportunities. Hence, in the process of allocating resources, the hypothetical competitive market system described in the previous chapters is likely to create temporary unemployment, and this unemployment is an essential part of the market process.

Permanent Unemployment
Prevented by Capital Markets

The major argument against the likelihood of sustained unemployment was based on an analysis of capital markets. The argument held that such unemployment was impossible because all incomes were either spent on consumer goods or services (thus maintaining demand for the labor producing those goods and services) or saved and all saving was turned into a demand for capital goods through private investment. Thus, there could be no decline in the money demand for goods and services and, *ceteris paribus,* there could be no decline in the demand for labor.

A crucial assumption in this argument was that all saving was reinvested. This assumption was based on a further assumption that the interest rate would fluctuate in such a manner as to make this occur. Fig. 5–1 illustrates this argument in the case of a hypothetical economy producing two goods—a consumer good and a capital good. Part a shows the production possibilities curve with the economy initially producing at position A (OC_1 consumer goods and OK_1 capital goods). Part b of the figure shows the consumer good market

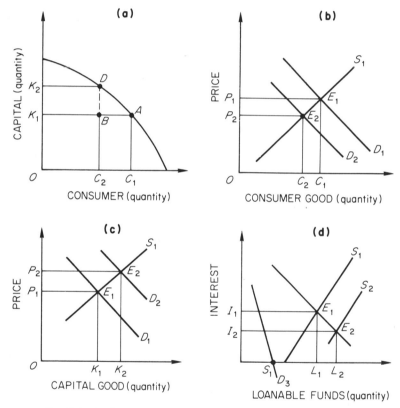

Fig. 5–1 Reallocation of Goods Production to a Full Employment Level

in equilibrium at position E_1 (intersection of D_1 and S_1). Part c shows the capital good market in equilibrium at position E_1 (intersection of D_1 and S_1). Finally, Part d of the figure shows the loanable funds market in equilibrium at E_1. As discussed in Chapter 3, this position equates the demand for loanable funds and the supply of loanable funds through fluctuations in the interest rate.

By assumption, the initial equilibrium positions jointly pick the full employment (full capacity) position A. The classical proof must show that, if shifts of one or more functions in one or more markets moved output to a position below the production possibilities curve, the loanable funds market would react in such a fashion as to move output back to the full employment level. Let us check for this property. Assume that because of changes in tastes and expectations the demand functions for consumer goods shift to the left. In the absence of compensating variations, this would lead to an output of OK_1 capital goods and OC_2 consumer goods, moving total output from A on the production possibilities curve to B below the curve. Hence, unemployment would result.

But compensating variations will occur in the loanable funds market. The decline in consumer good spending causes the supply of savings to increase since consumers must either spend or save. As a result, the schedule of the supply of loanable funds shifts to the right to S_2. This new supply schedule cuts the demand schedule at E_2, yielding an interest rate of IR_2. This new, lower interest rate stimulates borrowing by businessmen who use these funds to buy additional capital goods. Hence, the demand for capital goods shifts to D_2. This new demand schedule cuts the schedule of the supply of capital goods at E_2, producing an output OK_2 of capital goods. This increased production of capital goods moves output to position D on the production possibilities curve, and here labor is once more fully employed.

This is the basic process by means of which the neoclassical economists thought that the market mechanism would prevent permanent unemployment. Numerous objections can be raised to the assumptions behind this model, but we will confine ourselves to the most basic one. This is the assumption that the demand and supply curves in the loanable funds market intersect at a positive rate of interest and at full employment.[2] This need not be the case. The demand curve might cut the abscissa (horizontal axis) to the left of the point where the saving schedule starts to rise. The curve D_3 is an example of this. Such a result is possible only if some savings (the amount OS_1 in Fig. 5–1d) occurs at a zero rate of interest. In such a case, the loanable funds market does not produce an equilibrium rate of interest. Instead, what will happen is that the incomes of con-

[2] A superior method of analyzing this process is the aggregate demand-aggregate supply analysis currently emphasized in textbooks on macroeconomic analysis. See, for example, T. Dernberg and D. McDougall, *Macroeconomics,* 3d ed. (New York: McGraw-Hill Book Co., Inc., 1968).

sumers as a whole will decline, and this will cause the savings schedule to shift to the left. Eventually, the leftward shifting supply curve will intersect the demand schedule at a positive rate of interest, but this new equilibrium will be *below* the production possibilities curve.

Permanent Unemployment Prevented by Labor Market Adjustments

A second market mechanism, which the neoclassicists thought would prevent permanent unemployment, was wage and price cuts. This process is presented in Fig. 5–2, which represents the same economy as Fig. 5–1. Parts a and b of Fig. 5–2 present the capital good and consumer good markets; part c presents the market in which labor is hired for employment by capital good firms; and part d presents the market in which labor is hired for employment by consumer good firms. All four markets are initially in the equilibrium positions labeled E_1 and these together put the economy at position A on the production possibilities curve (shown in Fig. 5–1).

Now suppose that the demand for both capital goods and consumer goods decreases from D_1 to D_2. Tending to produce the new equilibrium positions E_2 (output of OK_2 in capital good market and OC_2 in consumer good market). As a result of this decline in output, the demand for labor on the part of both industries will diminish. The capital good industry's demand for labor will decline to D_2 (part c) and the consumer good industry's demand for labor will fall to D_2 (part d). In the absence of further changes, this would cause the quantity of labor services hired to fall from OL_1 in each market to OL_2 in both markets. But this unemployed labor will not be content with its unemployed status. These workers will offer their services at lower and lower wages until they all are hired again. Thus, in each market the supply of labor curve shifts down until it reaches S_2 where OL_1 labor is again being employed. Full employment has been restored but at lower money incomes.

This is not the end of the analysis, for adjustments are also being made in the product markets and are required if the lower incomes are to purchase to the full employment output in the capital and consumer goods markets. In both the consumer good and capital good markets, the decline in labor cost is reflected by a downward shift of the industry supply curve. This downward shift continues

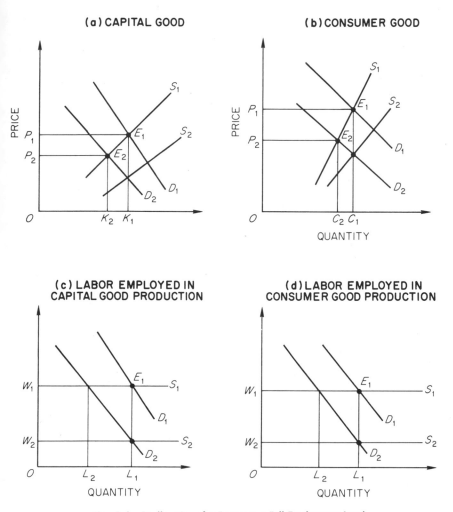

Fig. 5–2 Reallocation of a Factor to a Full Employment Level

until the original outputs are reestablished (OK_1 of capital goods and OL_1 consumer goods). (Supply curves shift to S_2.)

This neoclassical analysis overlooks one important interrelationship between the labor and the product markets. This is the fact that the product demand curves shift downward every time consumer income falls. Since every cut in the wage rate is accompanied by a decline in the income of laborers, every cut in the wage rate causes a decline in the demand for consumer and capital goods. This causes the demand for labor to decline in both markets (parts c and d). Hence, both the demand and supply curves shift down in the labor markets, and it is not certain that within the confines of this model full employment equilibrium will eventually result. That is, the demand curve might cut the horizontal axis to the left of OL_1 (full employment of labor) or the downward shift of the supply curve might be stopped at the "subsistence" level of wages, which might be above W_2.

This neoclassical analysis also makes a number of assumptions that are not valid for "modern" economies. One of the most important of these is that labor is supplied under perfectly competitive conditions and that products are sold in purely competitive markets. Once these assumptions are dropped the wage may fail to fall due to monopolistic control of the labor supply (for example, a labor union), and prices may fail to fall due to imperfect competition in the product markets.

Structural Unemployment
Prevented by the Loanable Funds Market

One type of unemployment that the preceding analyses did not consider is the so-called structural unemployment. This is a situation where unemployment exists in one sector of the economy while simultaneously jobs go begging in another or other sectors, and the unemployed labor does not obtain the available jobs because the jobs require skills that the unemployed do not have. This is a major problem in a rapidly growing economy characterized by technological change, which significantly changes the demands for various types of skills. How would the purely competitive market system solve this problem?

The answer is to be found in the loanable funds market. Assuming this market to be perfect; assuming the unemployed worker to be aware of the demand for various types of skills; assuming the laborer to be a utility maximizer, the typical unemployed worker would borrow the money needed to pay for skill training; with the acquired skills, the worker would obtain one of the unfilled jobs requiring the skill that he had just acquired. The income earned in this new employment would be sufficient to pay off the loan that had financed the education and to provide the worker with a higher standard of living than he had enjoyed while being unemployed. Thus, in the long run, the purely competitive market process solves the problem of structural unemployment.

BALANCE-OF-PAYMENTS EQUILIBRIUM

The final stability problem we will consider is that of dealing with fluctuations in the level of foreign exchange earnings. This problem is commonly known as the balance-of-payments problem. This problem is essentially an aspect of the more basic problem of resource allocation. Consequently, textbooks dealing with microeconomic theory never delve into the problem of trade. However, the purpose of this study is to give the student an understanding of the all-purpose nature of the market system as a decision-making device. Hence, a discussion of the ability of the market mechanism to solve the balance-of-payments problem is most appropriate. Furthermore, the insecurity created by the market process in solving this problem is so significant that it was noticed at the very beginning of the modern history of economic thought, and economists expressed approval of a public regulatory device (the gold standard), which mitigated this instability. Hence, it was in the area of international trade that modern economic analysis first acknowledged the shortcomings of the competitive market process.

Flexible Exchange Rates and the
Balance-of-Payments Problem

For the study of international economics, the properties of supply and demand schedules must be investigated further than they are in any general presentation. A particular property of a supply schedule is that it is also a demand schedule and *vice versa*. The reason that this statement may appear to be an anomaly is due to the fact of intervention of money between the two parties in the market place. Money serves as a medium of exchange as well as a unit of account. Consequently, for convenience, we normally calculate the price formed in markets in terms of a common denominator (unit of account)— money.

The price of a Ford as determined by the parties involved in the market may be $3,000, as conventionally illustrated by Fig. 5–3.

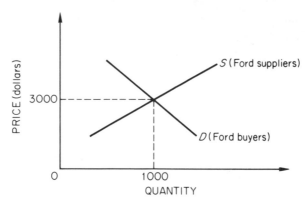

Fig. 5–3   Market for Fords

The price of each Ford is $3,000 and one thousand are bought and sold valued at $3,000,000.

However, this market may be represented in another way to give identical results. The buyers of Fords are required to have money as well as a taste for Fords, both of which are represented in the demand schedule. One has learned elsewhere that the amount of money buyers have certainly influences the position and shape of the demand schedule. That is, the supply of money offered by buyers is included in the demand schedule as influenced by their taste for Fords. Consequently, the buyers' demand schedule for Fords is also a suppliers' schedule of dollar offers for Fords. The Ford suppliers are offering autos for something they want (demand)—money—and the number of Fords offered depends on the suppliers' tastes for money and how many Fords they have to make their demands effective. As a result, we may represent the market alternatively to the above as represented in Fig. 5–4.

Looking at the market for dollars, we are now calculating the price of *each* dollar in terms of Fords. The parties to the market are reversed. The former suppliers are demanders, and the former demanders are now suppliers.

A dollar is worth 1/3,000th of a Ford and three million of them are bought and sold with Fords, which information we could also have gotten from Fig. 5–3. The slopes of the supply and demand schedules are conventional for conventional reasons. For example, the suppliers of dollars—people with money but without Fords—will part with more money if they can get a higher price, say 1/2,000th of a Ford. The demanders of dollars (Ford Suppliers) will, of course,

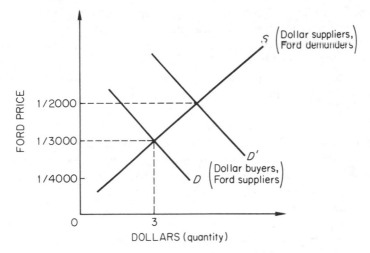

Fig. 5–4 Market for Dollars (in millions)

want more dollars if the price were lower, say 1/4,000th of a Ford. In other words, each schedule is really an offer curve, and the price in a market is the reciprocal of the price when you reverse the supplier and demanders.

If for some reason the demanders come into more wherewithal (Fords) to purchase dollars, their demand schedule is likely to be shifted to D'; and, given S, they are going to pay a higher price for each dollar (1/2,000th of a Ford). Understanding the above is important for the study of international economics and particularly for the markets where one currency is traded for another—foreign exchange markets.

In Chapter 1, an example of a market was given where Smith and Jones traded soap and candles to their mutual benefit. There it was pointed out that the principles involved in trading candles directly for soap were not altered by the use of money as a medium of exchange nor would they change if Smith and Jones used two different currencies. But this would complicate the exposition.

We can use our previous example in Chapter 1 by adding two currencies and a foreign exchange market preliminarily to studying some balance-of-payments problems.

Assume that Smith is now the United Kingdom and Jones, the United States. The United States will specialize in making soap, keeping some for consumption, and exporting some to the United Kingdom. The United Kingdom will now specialize in candle-making, keeping some for home consumption, and exporting some to the United States. *Again the price of a candle will never be as low as ⅘ nor as high as 1⅔ bars of soap to the buyer and seller.* But with our example now, we need to insert the phrase "domestic money" before the words price in the previous sentence.

The United Kingdom will calculate the price of soap and candles in terms of their own monetary unit, the pound sterling, while the United States calculates the price of candles and soap in terms of the dollar. As a simplifying measure, assume that the costs of production in each country for the production of soap and candles are constant, which would make their supply schedules horizontal or perfectly elastic.

Before trade, in line with our introductory example, assume that the price of a candle in the United Kingdom was £1 while the price of soap was £1¼. In the United States, assume the price of soap was $1 and candles cost $1⅔. The relationships are restatements of the original example in Chapter 1 where we assumed "time is money," that is, time measures cost. For example, if it takes five hours to produce the five candles in the United Kingdom while it takes five hours to provide four soaps, then *each* bar of soap costs 1¼ as much time as *each* candle.

With the above domestic prices in each country and a free exchange market, United States soap will be cheaper for the United Kingdom consumer than the domestic soap, and United Kingdom candles will be cheaper than United States produced candles to the American consumer. Again, both parties will benefit in specialization and exchange—this time in terms of cheaper money prices.

In order for the United States to purchase United Kingdom candles, the buyer, having dollars, must obtain pounds sterling, that is, buy sterling with dollars. The United States consumer cannot buy a pound for two dollars and then buy a candle in the United Kingdom for £1, for American candles only cost $1⅔; therefore, an American will not pay quite as much as $1⅔ for a pound. If an American pays $1 for a pound and buys a candle from the United Kingdom, the price is, of course, $1. The American would like it better if he paid 1 cent for £1, for then United Kingdom candles, while selling in the United Kingdom for £1, cost only 1 cent in American money. As in any market the seller of pounds has a lower limit and, in this case, that price is slightly above ⅘ or .8 of a dollar.

What the exchange rate will be depends on the supply and

demand conditions of the two commodities in the two countries; and since, in our example, we have assumed constant costs, demand conditions are paramount. All this can be represented by the usual supply—demand presentation of Fig. 5–5.

In Fig. 5–5, we have a situation where all markets are in equilibrium with given prices and quantities. For example, in the United States the price for a bar of soap produced in the United States is $1, with one hundred bars being sold to American consumers and one hundred bars to English consumers. The price is $1 to the American consumer and is £1 to the English consumer *only* because the exchange rate for £1 is $1. The price of English soap is £1¼ to English consumers and is $1¼ to American consumers; therefore, American and English consumers buy only American soap. The number of bars of soap exported by the United States and imported by the United Kingdom is one hundred while the value of American exports is $100 and United Kingdom imports is £100.

The United Kingdom demand for American soap, Fig. 5–5d, results in the English offering pound sterling for sale for dollars on the foreign exchange market, that is, in a supply schedule of English pounds in Fig. 5–5c. Here our buyer of a commodity must sell something (pounds) in order to get acceptable money (dollars) for the seller of the commodity. The combined demand for soap is D in Fig. 5–5a.

The original domestic prices for candles still prevails in both countries, that is, £1 and $1⅔; but the American plus English demand for candles results in an American demand for pound sterling in the exchange market, and, given the supply schedule of sterling, a price for £1 is $1. To the American consumer the price of one English candle then becomes $1.

The United States imports one hundred candles valued at $100 and the United Kingdom exports the one hundred candles valued at £100. In this trade of soap for candles, American exports and imports are valued at $100 while United Kingdom exports and imports are valued at £100. That is, each country has a balance of payments (trade) in equilibrium. Given our conditions, which include free markets, any change in the demand for the product of the other country will change the numbers of the product exported (imported) and the value of both the exports and imports of both countries but will always result in a balance-of-payments equilibrium. The mechanism through which these adjustments are made is the foreign exchange market.

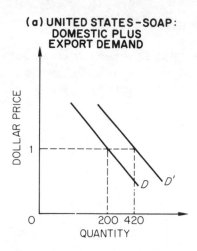

(a) UNITED STATES–SOAP: DOMESTIC PLUS EXPORT DEMAND

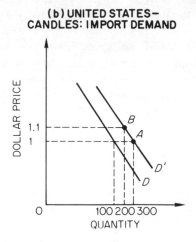

(b) UNITED STATES–CANDLES: IMPORT DEMAND

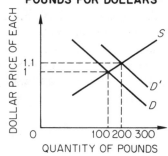

(c) FOREIGN EXCHANGE MARKET: POUNDS FOR DOLLARS

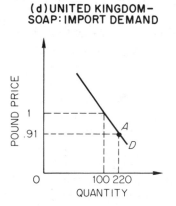

(d) UNITED KINGDOM–SOAP: IMPORT DEMAND

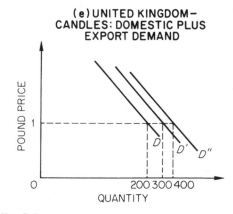

(e) UNITED KINGDOM–CANDLES: DOMESTIC PLUS EXPORT DEMAND

Fig. 5–5

To illustrate the above contention, let us say that national income of the United States increases. This will result in a shift to the right of the American demand curves for both soap and candles to D' in Fig. 5–5a and b. The shift to right of the demand curve for soap will not change the price for a bar of American soap paid by the American consumer, but it will change the *dollar* price of English candles. This is so because to obtain more English candles the American demand curve shifts for English exports to D' thereby requiring more pounds at the same pound price for each candle, part e. In order to obtain more pound sterling, the Americans must shift the demand schedule to D' in part c.

This demand shift results in a higher dollar price for the pound (a lower pound price for the dollar), which changes the dollar price of English candles to $1.1. Therefore, Americans will not want an *additional* two hundred candles as indicated by point A where the U.S. price is unchanged but will want an increase of only one hundred for a total of two hundred when the price is $1.1 (point B in part b). The American price for soap and the English price of candles are unchanged.

As a result of the changed demands, exports and imports of candles have changed both in numbers and value. Two hundred candles are now imported by the United States and exported by the United Kingdom. The value of English exports has risen from £100 to £200 while the value of American imports of candles has risen from $100 to $220.

The above has unbalanced our exports and imports (balance of payments), but this is not the end of the analysis. Although there has been a *change* in American demand, there has been no change in English demand but there is a change in the *quantity* demanded by the English of soap, for it is now lower priced in terms of pounds. In fact the exchange rate of $1.1 for each English pound means that a dollar bar of American soap now costs the Englishman only £1/1.1, or approximately £.91.

The English elasticity of soap import demand (and, thus sterling supply) is such that at the lower sterling price of American soap the English wish to now buy a total of 220 bars of American soap. This is a total outlay for English imports of £.91 × 220 = £200, which *exactly* matches their new level of the value of candle exports. The increased quantity of American soap demanded by the English is 120 bars or a total of 220, which the Americans have still priced at a dollar a bar; consequently, the value of American exports have risen to $220, which exactly matches their increased imports of candles.[3]

The original shift in demand by the Americans in the soap market called for the purchase of an additional 100 bars while the above described reaction lowered English price of American soap accounted for an addition of 120 bars wanted by Englishmen, making the combined increase in demand for American soap 220 bars.

Stabilizing Exchange Rates

The above case is an example of domestic and international markets responding to consumer direction in an *efficient* manner through a freely flexible exchange rate. Yet, it seems that the criterion of stability (security) was first most generally and consciously applied to the international prices in their markets. The rationale for applying this criterion arose from the fluctuations in exchange rates, which introduced an additional variable to international transactions as compared to purely domestic market transactions. Therefore, those that operated in the soap and candle markets needed to know the forces in those markets in addition to the forces in the exchange markets that did not arise solely because people wanted to buy and sell those two commodities.

People wanted to exchange dollars and pounds for other reasons such as to make investments in the other country, which could cause the exchange rate to change without there being any original disturbance in the demand for soap or candles but would result in changes in their prices calculated in their own currencies. That is, a shift in the demand for English pounds to D' as in Fig. 5–5 could arise because some Americans wanted to invest in England. This would change the American price of English candles as previously noted without there being a previous change of American demand in the candle market.

Among others, the above points out some of the reasons why commodity price instability existed in international markets and why a *fixed* exchange rate had appeal. For a long time the world has

---

[3] Note that Americans are not trading a bar of soap for a candle now. The terms of trade have changed to where the United States gives up 1.1 bars of soap for every English candle, and this is still within the limits of trading we originally established. This is not the final answer, however, since one would be required to analyze the income and substitution effects as between English and American purchases of soap and candles.

generally opted for fixed exchange rates, thereby applying the criterion of stability (security) instead of efficiency obtained through the flexible exchange market.

Since, with fixed exchange rates, the market adjustments cannot be affected through the exchange market, they must be made elsewhere. The general adoption of some form of gold standard with certain rules of conduct has meant that changes in domestic gold stocks would affect domestic prices and incomes in certain directions and amounts so that all markets would be cleared at the appropriate fixed exchange rate. The demonstration of this is not our task; our task is to briefly point out how some stability in international prices is to be achieved.

Say we have a situation where the United States fixes the exchange rate at $1 for £1. This means that, if a shift in supply (demand) in the foreign exchange market occurs, the United States government will shift the demand (supply) schedule just enough to offset it at the established exchange rate.

We can use our previous example to illustrate. Again, suppose we have an increase in United States income, which causes a shift in the import demand for candles to D' and a shift in the demand for sterling to D'. The United States authorities will then shift the supply of pounds to the right just enough to maintain the exchange rate by selling 100 English pounds. This means that the dollar price of English candles remains at 1 and the English pound price of American soap is still £1. Consequently, the American consumer will move to point A on D' for imported candles and will shift the total demand for candles in the English market to D'' instead of D' as in the previous example. The results will be that American imports of candles will be three hundred valued at $300 and English exports of candles will increase to three hundred valued at £300. English imports of soap will be unchanged since the price to them is unchanged, that is, the value of English imports is still one hundred bars of soap valued at £100. This means American exports valued at $100 are unchanged also. The United States now has an import trade balance and the English an export trade balance.

In order for the United States to shift the supply schedule of English pounds to the right, it must have some English pounds to do it or gold with which to buy them. This, of course, depletes the foreign exchange and/or gold reserves of the United States. A common definition of a balance-of-payments deficit involves and is measured by the loss of gold and/or foreign exchange. When countries have deficits for prolonged periods and dangerously deplete their foreign reserves, they must attempt to stop this erosion or reverse it.

The United States in this case could, through direct controls, limit the value of candle imports to the value of soap exports. If the United States does not do this, it could lower American domestic prices and/or incomes in order to get American consumers to purchase fewer candles and Englishmen to purchase more American soap.

By the adoption of a fixed exchange rate and foregoing efficiency, the United States obtained more stability (security) in international commodity prices but, in this case, created instability in the balance of payments and possibly in domestic prices and income.

SUMMARY

The economic objectives discussed in this chapter represent dimensions in which the competitive market process does not appear to perform well. Along with the personal security discussed in Chapter 2 and rediscovered in Chapter 4, the danger of mass unemployment and public unwillingness to let the price mechanism deal with balance-of-payments adjustment problems all have combined to bring about governmental intervention in actual market situations. Nevertheless, the problems associated with these goals can be resolved in good measure through monetary and fiscal policy, leaving ample scope for the market process. But there remains some conflict among performance norms (goals), and society often has to make choices as to the ranking and relative importance of the performance norm trade-offs.

6

The
Need
for Nonmarket
Solutions:
Market
Imperfections
and Public Goods

The preceding chapters analyzed the ways in which a perfectly competitive market system would solve various economic problems. Many students of the topic would argue that, subject to several qualifications, such a system does as good a job of making economic decisions as any alternative and that such a decision-making system should therefore be encouraged. This question of the extent to which decisions should be made through a competitive market process is clearly one of society's most important issues. The pragmatic answer varies from time to time and place to place, but there are certain basic principles that do not vary. Many of these principles were revealed in the preceding chapters. And, in general, the principles discussed in those chapters gave support to the market process. In the present chapter, we consider two phenomena favoring nonmarket decision-making: market imperfections and public goods.

MARKET IMPERFECTIONS

Market imperfections refer to those situations where one or more of the assumptions of the model of pure competition are violated. An obvious example is the case of monopoly (a single seller) or monopsony (a single buyer). A monopolist enjoys sufficient market power to restrict production and raise price so as to earn economic rent (excess profit). This rent is similar to the quasi-rent earned by competitive firms (see Chapter 2), but in the case of the monopolist there exist barriers to entry on the part of other firms.

Consequently, whereas the competitive firm loses its quasi-rent in the long run as a result of the entry of other firms, the monopolist maintains its monopoly rent in the long run.

The existence of monopoly vitiates the conclusion that the price and output determined by the market process represent a social optimum, for, unlike the perfectly competitive industry, the profit maximizing monopoly firm will not expand output and lower price to the point where marginal social benefits and marginal social costs are equal. In this case, therefore, governmental intervention may be required to improve market performance. The intervention might take the form of attempting to break up the monopoly and restore competitive conditions to the market. American antitrust laws are often cited as an example of this approach, although in practice those laws have rarely been used to break up existing monopolies. But there are cases where the antitrust approach encounters theoretical difficulties.

One theoretical reason for not attempting to restore competitive conditions is the existence of what are known as economies of scale. This refers to the situation where unit costs of production decline as the level of output of the firm increases. If the state of technology is such that these unit costs of production decrease throughout all the range of possible outputs, then one firm will always be able to produce the product at lower unit costs than will two or more firms. Hence, an antitrust policy that seeks to attack monopoly by breaking the firm up into a large number of competitors will end up creating a large number of higher cost firms.

This situation is known as the natural monopoly problem. Faced with this dilemma, public policy usually adopts one of two basic policy alternatives. On the one hand, the government can adopt the American approach of establishing a public regulatory commission to set prices and conditions of sale so as to approach a social optimum. On the other hand, the government can take over the firm and operate it as a public monopoly enterprise. But in either case, the natural monopoly problem calls for a partial replacement of the market decision process by a nonmarket governmental decision process.

Another theoretical argument for not attempting to restore competitive conditions is that *monopolistic* markets make up for their poor performance in terms of allocative efficiency by performing well in terms of innovation—the development and introduction of new technology and products. In this case, the argument applies both to monopoly and to oligopoly—the case where a small number of sellers occupies the market. In the oligopoly case, the firms are likely to behave monopolistically by fixing market prices and restricting output below the socially optimal level. But the same firms are likely to engage in rivalry with one another through such methods as the development of new products and production techniques.

If monopoly or oligopoly are to be maintained in order to promote innovation, there nevertheless exists a need for governmental surveillance and, where necessary, intervention in order to preserve minimally acceptable performance in terms of other performance norms. Hence, once again, there arises a case for nonmarket public decision-making processes to constrain the market process.

Monopoly and oligopoly represent situations where the market process cannot be relied upon to produce the allocative efficiency that we associate with perfectly competitive markets. The theories of monopoly, oligopoly, and a third market structure—monopolistic competition—are best approached using tools of analysis not developed in the present text. Hence, the reader is referred to any intermediate microeconomic theory text for a rigorous analysis of these market structures. For purposes of the present text, it is sufficient to note that in many cases market imperfections raise a question as to the desirability of interfering in the market process in order to improve economic performance.

EXTERNALITIES AND PUBLIC GOODS

The existence of market imperfections is not the only reason for favoring governmental intervention in the market process. A second important reason is the existence of a special type of commodity or service—the public good—which cannot be produced by the perfectly competitive market system at all or at least not in an optimal amount. The basis of the public good is the phenomenon of externalities. Hence, the place to begin the discussion of public goods is clearly with a consideration of the externalities phenomenon.

Externalities

Goods are usually defined in terms of their ownership. If the good is owned by an individual (or even by a group of individuals), it is characterized as his (or their) good. However, there are alternative approaches to this definitional problem. For instance, the good might be defined not in terms of ownership but in terms of the persons affected by it. For example, if Smith places shade trees on his side of the line adjoining Jones's property, not only would it be cooler in Jones's back yard, but the value of Jones's property would probably go up. The trees may be Smith's, but the effect of the trees is shared by both Smith and Jones. In fact, one can argue that it is the shade, the effect of the trees, that is valuable and not the trees themselves. And that is precisely the point. That is why the good in question is not really Smith's alone but is, in a sense, shared by both. However, one does not purchase shade. It is only trees that one finds for sale on the market, and thus it is trees that Smith bought. In common parlance, the trees are Smith's property, and Jones's property is treeless.

The economist recognizes the dilemma but at the same time bows to the common use of the English language and the realities of the market place. The economist would say that although the tree is owned by a single individual, it creates benefits for those other than its owner. These extra benefits are called *externalities*. Another way of expressing this is to say that the benefits of the shade tree are jointly supplied to both property owners. (If the benefits of the single tree were not jointly supplied, then we would have two separate goods that could be distinguished by, and sold separately in, the market.) Jointness of supply is thus a characteristic of externalities. However, our two property owners may have realized that the trees would jointly supply them with shade; and, being friends and easygoing types who both like shade, they would share the cost and therefore the ownership of the trees. In this case, there would be no externalities. Thus, the existence of externalities implies jointness, but jointness can exist without externalities.

The device of sharing the cost of the trees was a device by means of which the externalities associated with the trees were internalized. With joint ownership the trees could be treated as a pure private good, albeit one owned by two individuals rather than by one. There is, however, a second solution to this problem. If the tree owner had some way of charging his neighbor for the value of the shade, then the externalities would again disappear. Only if the tree owner (Smith) were unable to appropriate the value of the good to his neighbor would there be an externality to the neighbor. If Jones had to pay for it, then he would be purchasing something in exactly the same way in which one purchases any other strictly private good. Thus, the characteristic of nonappropriability is part of a true externality.

In the preceding example, the externality was positive. However, some externalities are negative—they cause harm instead of creating benefits. Automotive exhaust is jointly supplied with transportation. The atmosphere that is polluted is inhaled by individuals who do not own the car. Eliminating the externality, given the technological fact of exhaust being emitted from a running motor, would involve either cost sharing or appropriating the value of the effect. Since the exhaust is a negative good, cost sharing would involve the paying of a bounty to the new part owner. As in the case of the shade trees, both share in the cost of the good as they share in its benefits. The analysis is the same except for an algebraic change in sign. When the benefits received are positive, the costs are also positive; and when the benefits are negative, so are the costs.

Appropriability in our shade tree example meant that the receiver of the shade paid the owner of the shade tree a positive sum. In the automobile case, appropriability would mean that the receiver of the exhaust paid the owner of the automobile a negative sum. That is, the receiver of the exhaust was paid. In this second illustration, it is much more evident than in the first that sharing in the cost or appropriating the values of the benefits are, in the last analysis, the same thing. In both cases, there is an equation between the flows of cash and the flows of benefits, and, as with purely private goods, these flows will have opposite signs and will be distributed so as to be equal at the margin. Thus, the result will be an optimal allocation of these resources.

For the more business-oriented student, the concept of externalities can be restated in the terms of production functions. Smith is the recipient of an externality if his production function is influenced by the activity of another producer, Jones. It would cease to be an externality if Jones took this effect into account when determining his level of output. If Jones did not do so and if the externality had a positive effect on Smith's output, then, in terms of the interest of both producers, Jones would be underproducing, and thus the allocation of resources would be less than optimal. Smith, the recipient of the benefit of this externality, might induce Jones to expand his output by subsidizing Jones's operation; or, what is really the same thing, Jones would expand his production if he had the ability to appropriate the value of the benefits that he was providing for Smith.

The existence of externalities creates social benefits and costs that are not taken into account through the workings of an individualistic market process. Hence, there simply has to be some sort of nonmarket, group decision-making process to bring these benefits and costs into the calculations that ultimately determine the allocation of scarce resources. In the shade tree and production illustrations, there were only two parties involved, and it would not be out of the question for the parties to recognize their mutual interests and so internalize the externalities. But as the number of parties involved gets larger, voluntary action becomes less and less feasible. The only way producers of positive externalities could be enticed to expand (other than by governmental edict) would be payment of a subsidy, and the producers of negative externalities could likewise be induced to reduce output to the point where the marginal cost they bear is no less than what the society sacrifices only by a tax. Thus, the existence of externalities is a cause for governmental interference in the market process in the name of optimal allocation of resources.

Public Goods

In the discussions of imperfections and externalities, it was argued that the free play of market forces will not necessarily lead to a socially optimal allocation of resources. Public goods are an extreme case of this failure of the market place. These are goods that are valued by society and yet that would not be produced at all or at least would not be produced in sufficient quantities if reliance were placed solely on the workings of private markets. Now almost all private goods have public aspects (and, conversely, almost all public goods have private aspects). But the characteristics of what we will call a public good are sufficiently extreme to justify devoting a separate section of this chapter to the phenomenon.

In the case of purely private goods, the total consumption of the good is exactly equal to the sum of the consumption of the good by each of the individuals in the society. But in the case of the public good, the total consumption of the good is exactly equal to the consumption of the good by a single individual, and each individual's consumption of the good is equal to that of every other individual. Thus, in the private good case, an individual's consumption of the good is at the expense of someone else. What Smith has, Jones cannot have. But this is not so in the public good case. There is no diminution in the consumption of the good by one individual because of another individual's consumption.

It should be noted that the issue here is not that of socialism versus private enterprise. The concept of a public good is defined not in terms of whether or not the state or private individuals do the producing or financing. Instead, the distinction lies on the consumption side. The "public" in the case of the public good concept is the group that consumes the good (or, more precisely, the group that consumes the services provided by the public good). But what uniquely characterizes the good as a public good is not that it is consumed by large numbers of individuals (although this is a necessary condition). After all, a single animal produces the food for more than one individual, and a movie may be seen (consumed) by millions of persons. Yet these are called private goods, because, in spite of the fact that large numbers live off of a single animal or see a particular movie, it is possible to exclude the participants in either the feast or the movie simply by raising the price. In a strict sense, the case of a public good is one in which it is not possible to exclude any member of the public from consuming the good if the good exists. This is the *exclusion principle*.

National defense is commonly given as an example of a pure public good. If the nation is being defended, individual members of the nation are defended; and, conversely, if the nation is not defended, no member of the nation is defended. An individual member of the community cannot increase his share of national defense; and he can increase the quantity of national defense he receives only if the defense of the nation as a whole is increased.

Education is an example of an impure public good. It is a public good because of the prevalent view that all citizens are better off if the general level of education is high. But education also has strong private aspects. Up to a point, an individual's investment in his own education provides that individual with a greater income earning capacity that is uniquely his. This added income represents a return on the educational investment, which can be compared with potential returns on alternative investments. And there is little doubt that this return is high enough to cause a significant amount of education to be produced and sold on a private market basis if there were no governmental support of education. But it is equally clear that such private market-based education would be much more restricted than what can be observed under the publicly supported systems. Education is a case of a public good not because the private market approach would fail to produce any education but because the private market approach would fail to provide enough education.

It should be noted that in the case of the education example, the schools producing the education could be either public or private. The agency that produces the good and the agency that finances the good are completely irrelevant to the discussion. The existence of the American public school system in which the private aspects of education are publicly financed and the American private school system in which the public aspects of education are privately financed is testimony to the existing confusion among production, financing, and consumption. The financing arrangements follow from the nature of the good, which is defined in terms of its consumption. The agency that produces the good is determined on principles that have nothing whatsoever to do with whether or not the goods are public or private. In a socialistic economy, private goods are produced by nationalized industries; and, in a private enterprise economy, it would not be unnatural for public goods to be produced by private enterprise though financed by the public.

Finding the Optimal Amount of Public Good Production

There remains the problem of solving for an optimal allocation of resources when public goods are involved. As the preceding chapters indicated, this involves equating marginal social benefits and marginal social costs. This operation, in turn, requires the construction of demand and supply curves. And it is in the construction of the demand curves that the difference between private and public goods becomes clear.

In the case of private goods, the demand curve is obtained by the horizontal summation of individual demand curves. Each point on the market demand curve indicates the total quantity demanded by the community of consumers at a particular price. This point is obtained by adding the quantity demanded by each consumer at that price. If, for example, at a given price each of 100 consumers purchased X units of the commodity, then the total market quantity demanded would be $100X$.

In the case of public goods, such horizontal addition is inappropriate. The same unit of the public good can be consumed simultaneously by all members of the community. Thus, if at a given price the quantity demanded by each of 100 members of the community is X, then the production of X units will simultaneously satisfy all consumers. To produce $100X$ units as was done in the private good case would be wasteful since none of the consumers would consume more than X units and all consumers would consume the same unit. Thus, the horizontal addition of demand curves is clearly inappropriate in the case of public goods.

How, then, is a community demand curve constructed in the case of a public good? The answer, it turns out, is that the individual demand curves must be added vertically to obtain the community demand curve. This is illustrated in Fig. 6–1a where the community

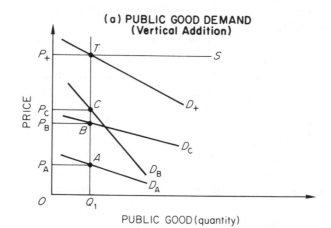

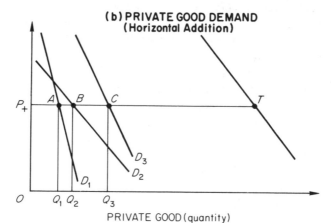

Fig. 6–1

demand curve, D_T, is obtained by vertical summation of the individual demand curves, D_A, D_B, and D_C. More precisely, at each possible quantity, the "price" points on the individual demand curves associated with that quantity are added vertically to obtain a community "price." For example, the quantity OQ_1 in Fig. 6–1a is associated with point A on demand curve D_A, with point B on demand curve D_B, and with point C on demand curve D_C. Adding these three points vertically, that is, adding the prices associated with these points, yields point T on the total demand curve. Put more precisely, adding prices P_A, P_B, and P_C yields price P_T, the price associated with point T on the community demand curve. The same procedure is followed for other possible quantities, and the result is the locus of points comprising the community demand curve.

For purposes of contrast, the construction of the private good market demand curve is presented in Fig. 6–1b. In this case, as noted above, the addition is horizontal. That is, a point on the market demand curve such as point T is obtained by adding the quantities associated with each of the individual demand curves at a given price. In this case, given the price P_T, the point on the community demand curve is obtained by adding the quantities OQ_1 (associated with D_1), OQ_2 (associated with D_2) and OQ_3 (associated with D_3) to obtain the quantity OQ_T with which the price P_T identifies point T on the community demand curve.

Contrasting parts a and b of Fig. 6–1, we can see that the difference between the market demand curve in the case of the private good and the community demand curve in the case of the public good is that the former is obtained through horizontal addition of the individual demand curves while the latter is derived by vertical addition of the individual demand curves. Another way of expressing this is that, in the case of the private good, each point on the market demand curve is found by starting with a given price and finding the total quantity that would be purchased, whereas in the case of the public good, we start with a given quantity and determine the total amount of money that consumers as a group would be willing to pay for that quantity.

Having derived a demand curve for the public good, we can now use simple supply and demand analysis to determine the socially optimal level of production. This is diagrammatically represented in Fig. 6–2 where D_T is the demand curve (analogous to D_T in Fig. 6–1a) and S is the supply curve. Assuming that the demand curve measures marginal social benefits and assuming that the suppy curve

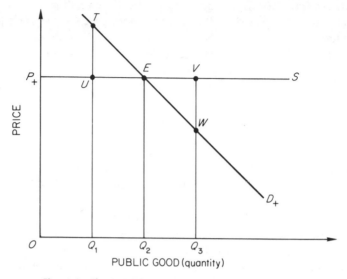

Fig. 6–2   The Optimal Quantity of Public Good Production

measures marginal social cost, the social optimum will be at the intersection of the demand and supply curves, that is at point E in Fig. 6–2. At any quantity less than that associated with this optimum point, marginal social benefits will exceed marginal social cost. Thus, at the output OQ_1, marginal social benefits (measured by the distance Q_1T) exceed marginal social cost (measured by Q_1U). And at any output greater than that associated with this optimum, marginal social cost exceeds marginal social benefits. Thus, in Fig. 6–2, the output OQ_3 involves marginal social costs measured by Q_3V and marginal social benefits measured by Q_3W. Since Q_3V exceeds Q_3W, this output represents excessive production from the standpoint of the social optimum.

Apportioning the Cost of the Social Good

There still remains the question of determining the proportion of the total cost to be borne by each consumer (who is also a tax-payer and will, in fact, pay through taxes). In the private good case, this problem is solved by each individual purchasing a quantity of goods determined by the intersection of the price line and that individual's demand curve. Multiplying this quantity by the price gives the proportion of the total cost of the industry's total output borne by that individual. The analogous solution in the public good case is to find the "price" charged each consumer by finding the point where that individual's demand curve cuts the vertical line, which is perpendicular to the quantity axis at the quantity representing the equilibrium level of output. Multiplying this "price" by the quantity (which all consumers utilize in the same amount) gives the individual's total contribution to the cost of producing the entire output of the social good. In Fig. 6–1a, for example, this solution would require that individual A pay the "price" P_A per unit of output of the social good. Individual B would pay the "price" P_B and individual C would pay the "price" P_C. Individual A's total tax bill would be $P_A Q_1$; individual B's total tax bill would be $P_B Q_1$; and individual C would have a tax bill of $P_C Q_1$. The sum of these three tax bills would be equal to $P_T Q_1$, the total cost incurred by the government in financing the production of OQ_1 of the social good.

As was the case with private goods, the argument that the intersection of the demand and supply curves represents a social optimum requires an assumption about the socially desirable distribution of income. In the case of the analysis of the preceding paragraph, the key assumption is that the proportional distribution of the tax burden should be the same as the proportional marginal satisfaction that each individual derives from the production and consumption of the last (marginal) unit of the social good. Since points on the individual's demand curve are assumed to measure this marginal satisfaction, the solution to the problem of distributing the tax burden, which was given in the preceding paragraph, is therefore optimal.

The Free Rider Problem

Having identified a method of finding the optimal level of production of a public good and having developed a rule for apportioning the cost of the public good among users, we now come to a vexing problem in the area of public good financing. This is the problem of inducing individuals to reveal their true preferences for public goods and services. This is not a problem in the case of private goods, because of the individual nature of the good. If an individual does not honestly reveal his preferences as shown by his willingness to "put cash on the line," then that individual will not receive the good or service. But this is not the case with public goods. Here, if the good exists, all individuals receive it; and the fact of whether or not an individual contributed toward the cost of production of the good (or the "purchase" of the good) is not a factor in that person's ability to consume the good. If the individual understates his demand, the total demand for the public good would, of course, also be understated. But if there are literally millions of other demand curves involved, then one individual's contribution toward the public good is an insignificant part of its total cost. And without this individual's contribution, the diminution of the total output of the good would be infinitesimal.

The role a single individual's tax dollars play in the cost of a social good may be negligible. But this same insignificant contribution may be a sizable part of that individual's income. Consequently, if the individual's payment for public goods is determined by his revealed preference for those goods, then the individual clearly has an interest in understating his preferences. The loss to the individual on the consumption side is small compared to his gain on the disposable income side. And if the size of the group that is involved in purchasing the public good is sufficiently large, as it is in the case of goods purchased by the national government, then the former loss approaches zero. As a result, each taxpayer as an individual has an interest in understating his preferences for public goods and therefore in obtaining a "free ride" at the expense of his fellow citizens. This is the *free rider problem.*

So far, this seems to be a moral issue. But the chances are that if one individual is perceptive enough to see this opportunity, then others will also realize the personal advantages of understating preferences. And if large numbers do this, then there really would be significant effects on the size of the output of public goods. Output would be too small, not in relation to the views of someone who constantly demands a greater role for government, but in relation to the true demand of the individuals who make up the society. Allowing each individual to pursue his self-interest results in a misallocation of resources; because in the case of public goods, self-interest consists of getting a free ride.

Thus, although the benefits of public good production may be greater than their costs at the margin and although all members of the community may recognize this, each person is still reluctant to increase his contribution for fear that others will not do likewise, forcing him to pay a disproportionate share of the total cost. If resources are to be optimally allocated, there is clearly a need for public intervention. That is why the size of public goods output and the structure of payments are imposed upon us by government. And that is why there are legal penalties for nonpayment of taxes. The legal penalties are simply the substitute for the penalties of nonconsumption that are imposed upon us by the market when we do not pay for private goods.

The Unanimity Principle

Although this may seem to be an obvious solution, it remains unsatisfactory to the economist. In the political realm, democratic procedure means that all are allowed to have their say; but, after all has been said, the majority rules. In the private goods market, total output is not what the majority wants but the sum of the desires of each of the members of the group. Thus, in a sense, one can say that decisions about aggregates are made unanimously, and it is this unanimity that results in the efficiency conditions being met for the individual as well as for the group. To the economic purist, there can be an optimal allocation of resources in the public good case only if the price-quantity relationships are determined on the basis of a *principle of unanimity*.

Unanimity is reached in the private goods sector by individuals adjusting the amount that they purchase to the market price, and this quantity demanded then feeds back to adjust the market price. Thus, there is a simultaneous determination of market price, market supply, and the quantity supplied and demanded by each individual. In this case, the market price is the price to the individual, and the market supply is the sum of the quantities supplied to each individual.

In the case of the public good, the market supply is the equal of the individual supply, and the market price is the sum of the prices paid by each individual. Thus, unanimity would imply that each individual adjusts his price to the market supply and the sum of these prices would then feed back to adjust supply. There would be simultaneous determination of market supply and price and individual shares of the total cost. The whole process would be perfectly analogous to the market solution, and the usual efficiency conditions would be met.

Knut Wicksell, a Scandinavian economist who worked on this problem in the late 19th century, actually proposed that this system be implemented through the parliamentary process. Instead of legislatures being asked to vote for or against a given tax or expenditure proposal, they would be given the opportunity of voting for packages that included a specific expenditure and a tax sharing scheme to finance it. By adjusting the tax sharing arrangements and coupling them with a variety of expenditure levels, Wicksell claimed, there would either be one package acceptable to all, or, if there were not, this would indicate that the society did not want the good in question at its supply price. Being realistic, Wicksell saw the possibility of an irrational legislator or even one that would act irrationally in order to blackmail his colleagues; and, therefore, he called for "virtual" unanimity rather than absolute unanimity.

As a concluding thought, we might note the symmetry between the analysis of the supply and demand for private goods and the supply and demand for public goods. In both cases there are distinct and independent supply and demand forces that interact to give us a price-quantity solution. The analysis on the supply side is the same for both types of goods. But the demand for public goods expresses itself as a tax contribution toward the purchase of the good while in the private good case it is the price of the good itself. And in neither situation could an optimal solution be expected if the forces of either supply or demand were monopolized. There has to be a truly simultaneous adjustment of the two functions, without one side having the power to force the other to meet its conditions. On the supply side, this means that monopoly (or indeed, anything less than pure competition) is inconsistent with optimality. On the demand side, in the private good case it means simply that the power of the monopolist buyer (called a monopsonist) is likewise unacceptable. In the public good sector, the equivalent of monopsony—the power to set a market price and so force supply to adjust to it—is the establishment of a tax structure to which public goods supply would have to adjust. Thus, the analogy with competition in the case of the public goods sector is the simultaneous determination of the tax structure and government expenditures. At the very least, it should be seen that these are two aspects of the same problem and that inefficiencies are bound to develop if decisions concerning the revenue side of the budget are made independently of decisions on government expenditures.

SUMMARY

Clearly, real world economies cannot rely entirely on the market system. The existence of market imperfections creates the danger of misallocation due to monopolistic market practices, and governmental intervention is required to eliminate this danger. Even in the absence of monopoly elements, there exists a need for governmental intervention in order to divert resources to the production of public goods. Indeed, even if it were decided that the maximum possible number of decisions should be delegated to the market, there would still be a need for governmental intervention to provide the institutional setting in which the market process thrives. Currency would have to be issued, ownership rights would have to be defined and enforced, standards of weights and measures would have to be established, traffic would have to be directed, and a host of other basic governmental functions would be required to assure the continued functioning of the competitive market process.

Yet decision-making through the political process creates many opportunities for resource misallocation. The free rider problem discussed above is just one of many problems besetting attempts to use the political process to identify the socially optimal pattern of resource allocation. For examples of others, the student need only consult the current issues of any daily newspaper.

Market decision-making and nonmarket decision-making are clearly complementary to some degree. But beyond that limited range of complementarity lies the vast range of situations in which market and nonmarket techniques are clearly substitutes for one another. Hence, a major issue facing every society is the extent to which nonmarket decision-making should be expanded into areas where the market is capable of making decisions.

Conclusion

At the present time, the world is witnessing an international trend toward comprehensive national economic planning. Developing countries are attempting to accelerate the growth and development of their economies through comprehensive planning. The developed nations of Europe, having used planning as a device to ward off the business cycle and promote steady growth, are now finding new socio-economic goals for the planners. And in the United States, the erratic application of monetary and fiscal policy, the increasing demand for social goods, and the dramatic recognition of such social costs of unregulated private enterprise as pollution may well combine to produce a concerted effort to install a comprehensive national economic planning system.

Those attracted to planning by its apparent orderliness and rationality often overlook the fact that market systems are also planning systems. And while market systems may seem chaotic to the untrained eye, generations of economists have collectively peered deep into the inner workings of the market mechanism and have discovered a truly coordinated system.

The preceding chapters have attempted to give the reader a fundamental understanding of this truly profound discovery without resorting to the numerous highly sophisticated tools of analysis that economists have developed. We have seen how the perfectly competitive market "planning system" simultaneously pursues such economic objectives as the efficient allocation of resources, economic growth, a "fair" distribution of income, and balance-of-payments equilibrium. We have also noted the difficulties that such market systems are likely to encounter in terms of the goals of personal security, full employment, and the optimal allocation of scarce resources to public goods.

Students who have come this far and wish a deeper understanding of the structure and functioning of market systems must now proceed to three distinct bodies of literature. First, of course, there is the literature of microeconomic theory. Any intermediate microeconomic theory text will provide the student with a kit of more sophisticated analytical tools, which will sharpen the understanding of the topics discussed above. Armed with these additional tools, the student can then plunge into the vast literature in the field.

Second, for further understanding of the public problems in economics, the student could consult any intermediate textbook in the applied branch of economic analysis known as Public Finance. A work directed at the specific problem of public goods is Professor Buchanan's *The Demand and Supply of Public Goods*.[1]

Third, there is a vast literature dealing with the actual workings of modern economies with their high incidence of imperfectly competitive markets. Within the discipline of economics, this literature can be found in a number of specialized fields such as: Industrial Organization and Public Policies Toward Business, Labor and Manpower Economics, and Agricultural Economics.[2] Outside of the formal discipline of economics, the student can consult the specialties taught in most business schools (university level) as well as in the other social sciences. In addition, there exists a vast popular press catering to the business community and its observers and cranking out a large volume of short articles dealing with business firms, industries, factor markets, capital markets, and public policies toward business. A visit to any university library will enable the student to locate a large sample of such publications.[3]

To comprehensively cover all these additional sources of information on the workings of market systems is clearly a task beyond

[1] James M. Buchanan, *The Demand and Supply of Public Goods* (Chicago: Rand McNally, 1968).

[2] The best method of finding areas of possible interest within the discipline is to consult the following three reference works: the *Index of Economic Journals,* prepared under the auspices of the American Economic Association; the *Journal of Economic Literature,* published by the American Economic Association; and Ralph L. Andreano, Evan Ira Farber, and Sabron Reynolds, *The Student Economist's Handbook* (Cambridge, Mass.: Schenkman Publishing Co., 1967).

[3] The book by Andreano, Farber, and Sabron will also guide the student to this literature.

the capacities of a single individual. But armed with the basic framework provided by this text as well as that afforded by good intermediate microeconomic theory text, most students will be able to read selectively and by so doing will steadily acquire a deeper understanding of the nature what some would call the most effective planning system yet devised by man—the market system.

Index

Absolute advantage, 9
Agriculture, 64
Andreano, R., 133
Antitrust laws, 117
Appropriability, 119–20
Auction, 41

Balance of payments, 105, 109–11
Baldwin, R., 96
Buchanan, J., 133

Capital formation, 47–56
Caves, R., iv
Circular flow, 45–47
Cobweb model, 37–41
Communications, 10
Comparative advantage, 9
Comparative statics, 54–57
Consumer surplus, 95

Demand curve, 21–22
Derived demand, 69–73
Derived marginal revenue, 70–71
Dutch auction, 41
Dynamic adjustment process, 25–27, 29–32, 51–54, 76–84

Economies of scale, 117
Efficiency, 33–36
Equilibrium, 23–24
Equity, 33
Exclusion principle, 122
Externalities, 118–21

Farber, E., 133
Firm, business, 10–11

Flexible exchange rates, 112
Foreign exchange market, 105–12
Free rider problem, 127–29

General equilibrium, 28–29
Gold standard, 105, 113
Growth, 21, 33, 44–60

Imperfections, market, 116
Income distribution, 68–96
Index of Economic Journals, 133
Industrial organization, 133
Innovation, 57, 118
Interest rate, 47–49, 85–88
Investment, 45–47

Joint supply, 119
Journal of Economic Literature, 133

Loanable funds market, 47–53, 99–101

McDougall, D., 102
Marginal physical product, 70
Marginal social benefits, 34
Marginal social costs, 34
Market, 2, 8, 10
Marketing, 9–10
Marshall, A., 27
Massel, M., ii
Meier, G., 96
Money, 11–13
Monopoly, 116–18, 130
  natural, 117
Monopsony, 116, 130

Oligopoly, 117–18
Opportunity cost, 18–20, 22

Partial equilibrium analysis, 21–32
Performance norms, 33
Personal security, 33, 36
Planning, 132
Production possibilities curve, 17–21
Profit, 93–94
Public finance, 133
Public good, 121–23

Quasi-rent, 25–27

Rent, 69, 88–93
  differential, 90
  scarcity, 90
Reynolds, S., 133
Ricardo, D., 68
Robinson, J., 72

Saving, 46, 49–51
Schumpeter, J., 57
Smith, A., 2
Specialization, 2–10
Stability, 33, 97–114
Supply, 22–25
  long run, 23
  short run, 24
  very short run, 24
Static analysis, 29

Tatonnement, 41
Taxes, 126–30
Transportation, 10

Unanimity principle, 129–30
Unemployment, 19, 98–105

Wages, 69, 73–85
Wicksell, K., 130